BRCA mutation. Amy Byer Shainman shares her in-depth personal perspective, as well as, a 360° panoramic perspective from physicians, genetic counselors, and loved ones that add texture to her story and her journey."

—*Shera Dubitsky, MEd, MA, Senior Advisor Sharsheret*

"More than a memoir, it is an essential resource for women concerned about breast cancer and all that it entails, both before and after a diagnosis. Sources and resources listed at the end of the book provide vital help to those seeking further information."

—*Foreword Clarion Reviews*

"It is a book to learn from but also an account to enjoy on a personal level. Beautifully written and interestingly presented through a central structural metaphor, it is a biography dealing with an increasingly important topic, and one that will appeal to a very wide audience."

—*Readers' Favorite*

"Amy Byer Shainman has pulled back the curtain on what it's like to carry a BRCA gene mutation. Nurses, interested in oncology, will find this book informative as they will likely become more enlightened as to what their patients are going through."

—*Iris R. Accettola, MSN, RN, OCN (retired)*

"With raw honesty, Shainman articulates coming to terms with her decision to have a prophylactic 'preventative' mastectomy. Whether she is reflecting on the value of heeding intuition, documenting a surgical consultation, or dealing with anger, Shainman transparently tells it like it is. I recommend the book to readers who want to learn more about hereditary cancer, genetic counseling, and the BRCA gene."

—*OnlineBookClub.org*

"Resurrection Lily is an applause worthy memoir that will affect its audience in deep and unexpected ways."

—*Feathered Quill Book Reviews*

"Told with a brutal honesty, while still maintaining the occasional foray into lightheartedness of everyday life, Resurrection Lily resonates with as much inspiration as it does information. As a guide to monitoring one's health and remaining vigilant for any possible detriments to that health, this story should be recommended reading for anyone with a genetic makeup and breast tissue – meaning, of course, everyone."

—*IndieReader*

"Phenomenal memoir. This book has a well of information laced throughout it. It is well researched and supported. This book is an invaluable tool to anyone who is on their own BRCA journey."

—*Shannon H. Pulaski, Esq. Patient Advocate, Author of Mom's Genes*

"My rating, 5 out of 5 stars...an informative and interesting book about hereditary cancer, with loads of practical advice and information on where to get help and guidance."

—*EmmabBooks.com*

"A Very Moving Read! Resurrection Lily is a compelling account of the author's experience of coming to grips with the knowledge she carries a BRCA1 gene mutation. The voices of her sister, a dear friend and beloved grandmother are 'heard' throughout as the author writes tenderly about each of them. Five Stars!"

—*Nancy Stordahl, Author of Cancer Was Not a Gift & It Didn't Make Me a Better Person, Educator, Blogger, nancyspoint.com*

"Resurrection Lily realistically and meaningfully captures the essence and nuances of what women face when living with a

"Beautifully told and incredibly researched. This book explains what the BRCA gene is and all its ramifications in incredible detail which could be incredibly boring except that Shainman weaves the medical and scientific information into her personal story. Written with authenticity and a generous dose of humor…a wonderful memoir and a great resource of BRCA information."

—*Valerie Staggs, Founder pandoraskids.org,*
Author of This Side of Heaven

"The amount of knowledge and access to resources is priceless… lives will be saved."

—*Reader Views*

"5 out of 5 stars. Simply put, this book might save your life, and because of that fact, to me, it is a 'No-brainer.' You should not only want to read this book, you NEED to read this book."

—*Amie Gaudet,*
Amie's Book Reviews, amiesbookreviews.wordpress.com

2019 Independent Author Network Non-Fiction Book of the Year

2019 Independent Author Network Award Health & Medicine Book

2019 IndieReader Discovery Award Health & Medicine Book

2019 FAPA President's Award Health Book

2019 Reader's Favorite Book Award Non-Fiction/Genealogy Book

2019 Best Book Award American Book Fest, Science

2019 Independent Publisher Book Award Best Adult Non-Fiction E-Book

2019 SPR Book Award Honorable Mention, Shortlisted for Excellence

RESURRECTION
—— LILY ——

RESURRECTION
—— LILY ——

The *BRCA* Gene, Hereditary Cancer
& Lifesaving Whispers from
the Grandmother I Never Knew

AMY BYER SHAINMAN

ARCHWAY
PUBLISHING

Archway Publishing books may be ordered through booksellers or by contacting:

Archway Publishing
1663 Liberty Drive
Bloomington, IN 47403
www.archwaypublishing.com
1 (888) 242-5904

ISBN: 978-1-4808-6706-2 (sc)
ISBN: 978-1-4808-6708-6 (hc)
ISBN: 978-1-4808-6707-9 (e)

Library of Congress Control Number: 2018956639

Printed in the United States of America.

Archway Publishing rev. date: 12/04/2019

For Lillian,
Kristin,
Sista,
and Jon, Brooke, and Ben

Contents

PART I: SOIL, SEEDS, AND LEAVES

PART II: LILIES

PART III: SUNLIGHT AND SHADE

PART IV: PERENNIAL PATIENT

PART V: REFLECTION POND

PART VI: HONEY AND HORNETS

PART VII: HAMPERED HEALING GARDEN

PART VIII: REPURPOSED FLOWERS

PART IX: GARDENERS

PART X: BUTTERFLIES AND BLOOMS

Preface

What if I told you that the airline just tested the airplane you are in and they found that it has as high as an 85 percent chance of crashing? What if the airline could reroute you and give you another option? Although that other option might be a difficult trip, it may just save your life. What would you do? Would you tempt fate with such a high risk of crashing? Would you even want to know this information about your airplane and the possibility of crashing?

Now I am going to rewrite the above paragraph, replacing the words *airplane, airline,* and *crashing* with the words and phrase *body, doctors,* and *breast cancer,* respectively.

What if I told you that the doctors just tested the body you are in and they found that it has as high as an 85 percent chance of developing breast cancer? What if the doctors could reroute you and give you another option? Although that option might be a difficult trip, it may just save your life. What would you do? Would you tempt fate with such a high risk of breast cancer? Would you even want to know this information about your body and the possibility of breast cancer?

I use the airplane analogy to illustrate the emotional complexities presented to a woman who carries a *BRCA* gene mutation. Women with a *BRCA1* or *BRCA2* gene mutation have as high as an 85 percent chance of developing breast cancer.

Everyone is born with two *BRCA1* and two *BRCA2* genes, and when you are born with a *BRCA1* or *BRCA2* gene mutation, one of those *BRCA1* or *BRCA2* genes, also known as tumor-suppressing genes, is not working. Therefore, you only have the protection of one working gene. Hence, people with a *BRCA1* or *BRCA2* gene mutation inherently have an increased risk of certain cancers. Although there are different ramifications for men, men can also carry and pass on a *BRCA1* or *BRCA2* gene mutation to daughters and sons.

My passion for *BRCA* education, support, and advocacy began in 2009 after I first learned about hereditary cancer and *BRCA1* and *BRCA2* gene mutations from my sister. My sister, diagnosed with both ovarian cancer and uterine cancer (two separate primary cancers) in 2008, found out that she had a *BRCA1* gene mutation more than a year after her diagnoses. *BRCA1* was first discovered in the laboratory of Dr. Mary-Claire King in 1990, it was cloned in 1994, and widespread clinical genetic testing for both *BRCA1* and *BRCA2* became available in 1996. So, why were healthcare providers and my family unaware of *BRCA* mutations at the time of my sister's initial diagnoses?

"About 1 in 500 to 1 in 800 individuals has a *BRCA1* or *BRCA2* gene mutation, and gene mutations are more common in specific ethnic groups. For example, men and women of Eastern or Central European Jewish descent, specifically Ashkenazi Jewish descent, have approximately 1 in 43 chance of having a *BRCA1* or *BRCA2* mutation."[1]

After learning more about hereditary cancer and *BRCA* gene mutations, I knew I could not live with myself if I remained silent about the information. Having these pearls of lifesaving wisdom continues to compel me to help people connect the dots and possibly save lives. When I started to journal about my experience in 2010, that's when I got the initial idea to write a book.

Since 2008, the genetic landscape has evolved regarding *BRCA* awareness, test accessibility, and research. In 2013 and 2015, movie star and humanitarian Angelina Jolie shared her *BRCA* story, garnering global media attention. In 2013, the Supreme Court of the United States ruled against the patenting of human genes, which in turn caused competition to occur in the genetic testing marketplace. Scientific advancements and new treatments *are* happening, but there is still a long way to go. We who have hereditary cancer syndromes need access to better options to protect our health.

I hope that soon there will be research that provides less invasive cancer risk reduction options for women than having to undergo mastectomy and ovary removal. Yes, I want better options for my daughter. However, until those discoveries are made, men and women will continue to have to make challenging decisions surrounding their increased risk of cancer.

And this leads to my story. I hope you come to understand *BRCA* and hereditary cancer syndromes through the expert commentary and the patient experiences. I believe that what I have shared will be a source of comfort and help for individuals and families with similar issues and a source of insight for other readers.

A few names and details have been changed or omitted for privacy reasons; a few details have been edited for clarification. It is important to note that every medical situation is deeply personal and highly patient specific. It is vital for you to do your own research and consult with your own medical professionals. To ensure you make the best health care decisions for yourself, please speak with a certified genetic counselor before and after any genetic testing.

Amy Byer Shainman

The resurrection lily is a free spirit of the plant world. Each plant has a mind or personality of its own, blooming where it wants, when it wants, and doesn't bloom if it so chooses. Parts of the plant are toxic. The foliage, which can become rather lush, eventually dies back, without any sign of bloom. Weeks, and even months, may pass, and all may have been forgotten. Then, seemingly overnight—thin, naked and pink stalks emerge from the ground—and within a few days it is covered with lovely, lily-shaped blossoms.'
—*an anonymous gardener*

Prologue

Dear Lillian,

Thank you. Because of you, I am here. I'm so grateful to you for everything that I have.

Your struggles have helped save my life. Your experiences have saved my sister's life.

I share your story every chance I get.

Your journey continues to have an impact on my children too, because your story is my story. Well, sort of; not exactly.

I admire your style, grace, and joy. Those qualities, plus your luminous porcelain skin, jump out of the beautiful photos of you that I have hanging on the wall going up my staircase. I know Dad loves the picture of you sitting in the Adirondack rocking chair in the garden; it sits on his desk in his home office. In that photo you are wearing what looks like a favorite hat, just slightly shielding your pale skin from the sun—and, might I add, you are looking quite fashionable! In many of the pictures, you are wearing hats. I love that! I have a collection of about twenty different hats! It's when I am wearing a hat that I think of you most. Is the reason behind our mutual love of caps to make a fashion statement, to cover up bad hair days, or to shield our fair skin from the outside sun? For me, it can be all three. I sense for you it was mostly a fashion statement, with maybe just a bit of shielding yourself from the bright sun.

I do think I look like you in some of those old photos—especially the sepia-colored picture where you are sixteen years old. Just today, a good friend was over, saw the photo sitting on my desk, and said, "Wow, those are your eyes!" I think Jan has your smile.

Anyway, if only you were close by so we could have dinner and chat. I would very much like that. But I know that's not possible; you are too far away. However, I feel you by my side. So I am writing to you, writing for you, writing with you. You are my strength, you are my comfort, and you continue to be my guide. As I said, your story is also my story—well, it is, but not exactly.

It would have been wonderful to have known you, hop up on your lap, feel your warmth, and have you spoil me. I am sad I won't be able to do that—ever—and I often get sad for my dad, who was only able to do that until he was seven years old.

However, I always think of you with love and honor. You are now forever a part of me. Thank you for being there for me. I have felt your quiet whispers and subtle urgings. These feelings have become my intuition and my comfort, and they are with me in every decision I make. Because of you and your guiding spirit, you and I have been able to have a relationship. It may not be the "typical" relationship that both of us wanted, but it is there, and it is powerful.

You have helped make it so I will not be lying beside you anytime soon.

Lillian, I have felt your energy sweetly and consistently elbowing me to share our story. Your nudges have been loud, and I have heard you. "Amy, please make my life mean something. Use your voice, press forward, share my story, our story, and save lives, save others—it's the right thing to do."

So this is for you, Lillian, for our family, for all families, and for the future generations of all families everywhere.

Love,
Amy, your granddaughter

PART I

SOIL, SEEDS, AND LEAVES

CHAPTER

1

Resurrection Lily

*D*ad, *seriously? How can one person accumulate so many boxes of crap!* That's what was going through my head as I opened the door to Dad's home office closet. Thankful all the stuff inside did not come tumbling out on top of me, I wasn't exactly sure what I was searching for; there was just the feeling to investigate that closet while I was home visiting my parents.

Old photos were sticking out of one box, so I began there. Sifting through these pictures was very moving for me. I loved seeing my dad as a little boy—all the black-and-white photos plus the sepia ones of him as a little boy with his parents. Dad's parents, as well as my maternal grandparents, died long before I was born, so learning anything about either set of grandparents was both exciting and fascinating for me. Seeing all of these hidden treasures of Dad's childhood, I wondered why he never shared them with me before.

As I looked at all the great memories in front of me, I thought it would be an excellent idea to make Dad a scrapbook for his seventy-fifth birthday, which was later that year, August 2002. My daughter, Brooke, was only six months old, so I knew I would have time to sort through everything after I put her to sleep. I was sure if I kept at it for a few nights, I would be able to get through all Dad's stuff.

One evening while sorting, I came across a piece of paper about my dad's mother, Lillian, my paternal grandmother. However, the flowery verbiage of 1934, plus the decayed quality of what seemed to be a letter, made it extremely hard to read, almost illegible. It appeared to be a medical letter. I knew my grandmother Lillian had passed away when she was very young, at only thirty-three years old. As I attempted to read, I paused briefly on a word—*metastatic*. The overall message seemed to be about Lillian having an illness, but I couldn't make out most of the words, and I wasn't sure what *metastatic* meant. It didn't faze me too much, as I didn't mention that word or even the letter to either my parents or my husband, Jon. I was enjoying all the photos and focusing on my new scrapbook project for Dad's birthday and mostly on keeping it a surprise.

A year later, when I was back home at my annual ob-gyn exam, I felt compelled to insist on having a baseline mammogram at age thirty-four, even though the recommendations in 2003 were to start yearly mammograms at age forty.[1] Something seemed to be pushing me to insist on getting a mammogram—something in my subconscious. You can call the feeling woman's intuition, the sixth sense, or that inner voice Oprah Winfrey is always talking about: the whisper on your shoulder. Some people call it universal energy, after-death communication, or even having an angel.

So, I had the mammogram. Results: mammogram normal.

I had another distinct overwhelming feeling after my son Ben was born in June 2004. The feeling hit me right as Jon wheeled me out of the hospital. I thought, *Wow, I think this is the last baby I am going to have.*

Why was my intuition telling me that? I'd always thought I would have at least three kids.

So, while I was beyond joyful with Ben's arrival, I had a deep sadness upon leaving the hospital, a bizarre feeling of sorrow and mourning so oddly contradicting my ecstatic newborn euphoria just ten seconds before Jon wheeled me out. My intuition told me it wasn't postpartum depression. It was *the feeling*.

CHAPTER

2

Root Feeling

All I know is that I don't know.
—Socrates

I distinctly remember the first time I had the feeling.
As I stood in right field watching my third-grade classmate gear up to nail the yellow kickball, unknown energy raced through me, and in that instant, I knew the ball was going to come directly to me and I was going to catch it.

In high school, I had the feeling when I dreamed that the mother of an old friend from middle school was in the hospital. The feeling seemed so random that I was compelled to awkwardly approach my acquaintance from middle school in the busy high school hallway the next day.

"Hey," I said. "How are you? Um, I just have to ask: Is—is your mom okay?"

"No," she said. "My mom is in the hospital."

Intuition, coincidence, synchronicity, serendipity, spirituality? What was this? Telepathy? Can someone inherit "telepathy"?

According to neuroscientist, psychiatrist, and author of *The ESP Enigma: The Scientific Case for Psychic Phenomena*, Diane Hennacy Powell, MD, experiments have shown that most psychic experiences occur when sensory organs are muted, such as when we're dreaming or having a near-death experience. She says genetics are likely behind it and that it runs in families. If you talk to psychics, she says, they'll tell you there's a family history of psychic ability and that, although we haven't found it, there's likely a gene for it. Powell says there are also cases where people haven't had any psychic abilities until they've suffered head trauma. She says what's common is that for these people who've had this head trauma, the structure and function of their brain has been changed. They're often not able to function very well in the real world because they don't know how to use the analytical side of their brain.

Well, I did have a significant head trauma when I was five years old. I was roughhousing with my older brothers and rammed the back of my head into a sharp corner of a wall. The injury resulted in my long curls being shaved off to a short pixie and my receiving stitches across the back of my head. Also, I completely sucked at analytical math. Math beyond eighth grade—forget about it. In my freshman year of college, I failed the math equivalency test but thankfully was able to graduate because my alma mater decided to get rid of the math requirement.

Dr. Powell also says that many people have precognitive experiences—mainly through dreams—on a regular basis. She relies on studies that reveal how some precognitive dreamers have even saved their own lives by retrieving information from a future that already exists.[1]

Is it possible I inherited the feeling from my mom? Was it genetics?

Over the years, Mom has told me eerie stories of things happening between her and her identical twin sister, my aunt Marilyn. For three years straight, they both sent my older sister, Jan, the same exact birthday card. Another year, they mailed each other the same birthday gift—the unusual combination of an umbrella and a woman's slip. Still, to this day, they pick up the phone to dial each other at the same time. However, I've heard about telepathy or a psychic connection between twins.

The idea of twin telepathy has been around for well over a century. Telepathy is the process of assessing thoughts or feelings without help from sensory input such as sight, sound, or touch. Many identical twins—perhaps as many as one in five—claim to share a special psychic connection. According to experts, however, despite decades of research trying to prove telepathy, there is no credible scientific evidence that psychic powers exist, either in the general population or between twins specifically.[2]

Pamela Prindle Fierro, who is an author and the mother of twins, has written about twins and telepathy and says there is plenty of anecdotal data to support the idea. Nearly every set of twins can relate a story. Despite the lack of scientific proof, it is generally accepted that such incidents are signs of a deep emotional connection that produces an intense sense of empathy, strong enough to generate physical sensations, such as feeling pain when a cotwin is hurting.[3]

However, I am not a twin. But could it still be possible I inherited something deep inside my DNA besides Mom's short stature and wavy hair? Was there a possibility that Mom had nothing to do with the feeling and that I'd inherited this from Dad? After all, I did get Dad's hands and fair skin.

All I know is that I don't know.

What I do know is that throughout those unpredictable and sometimes tumultuous phases of childhood, puberty, and college, and into adulthood, I continued to experience the feeling. I like to think of it as a powerful gut instinct, a positive intuitive force guiding me in specific directions, always seeming to keep me safe and to have my best interests at hand. Some of these feelings have been not only a guiding force but also inexplicable and, yes, even lifesaving.

CHAPTER

3

Blossom

I was moody, apparently. Mom; my sister, Jan; and I were all in Mom's dressing area looking at some of Mom's new clothes. The two of them, however, were in their own world, talking back and forth in chitter chatter and glances. They did this while holding up clothes to their bodies in the mirror as if I were not even in the room. I finally snapped when I heard them whisper my name. "What!" burst out of me. I was very irritated at the two of them because they were now talking about me and not to me.

"You are moody for sure," my sister responded, which was followed by more annoying eyebrow lifts and nods. She continued, "We are talking about your period, your time of the month."

And Jan and Mom were right. My period came exactly a week later on a Sunday morning, right before religious school, which started around eight thirty. I was eleven years old and was now officially the second sixth-grade girl whom I knew of to get my period.

I ran out to the kitchen that Sunday morning. "Mom, I think I got 'it.'" She reacted calmly but assertively and started busily opening and closing different drawers, looking inside for something she couldn't seem to find. She finally reached up into the back of a tall cupboard. As she handed me a pile of gauze, she said, "You know, you were the tallest person in your fifth-grade class, Amy, the center back of that fifth-grade class photo; you got your height early. Here—put this gauze in your underwear."

I knew what a period was, right? At least I thought I did. I knew that girls got this thing called a period. It came once a month, and it was a period. I mean, I thought it was a period, literally like the "dot at the end of a sentence" period. Mom had given me the gauze to put in my underwear for my period, which was only going to be a period of blood, just a dot of blood.

Apparently, getting one's period and feeling yucky wasn't reason enough to stay home from religious school, because the next thing I knew I was in Dad's car and he was driving me there. I felt awful that whole morning. Why did they make me go to Sunday school? Cranky and feeling terrible, I couldn't wait to get home. This period, I did not like what it was doing to me.

The minute I walked in through the door to the house, I ran to the bathroom to go check on my period. "Ahhhhh!" I shrieked as I pulled down my underwear, perplexed and embarrassed. The gauze was soaked!

You've gotta be kidding me? Totally grody! The period is way more blood than just a dot!

While I was at Sunday school, Mom had gone and bought me some Stayfree maxi pads, and now she was showing me how to use them. I was going to need them because, supposedly, my body was going to bleed for several days and not just produce a dot of blood. I guess I was now officially a woman at age eleven. But I didn't feel like a woman. I attached the pad to my underwear, which still read "Carter's." What is a woman supposed to feel like anyway?

I was feeling shy and insecure and most definitely was not standing up to those "mean girls." There were mean girls in creative dance class, and they were always cutting in front of me when we had to line up for "color" dancing. In color dancing, the teacher would yell out a color and, one at a time, each of us would dance the interpretation of that color. Every time I would dance, the mean girls would be whispering among themselves, imitating how I would dance to that color. One day as I was dancing to the color yellow, they were making particular fun of me; I had my arms stretched out and waving around, bopping my head left and right, with a big cheesy smile, interpreting yellow as if I were the sun. I looked ridiculous. But we all did. They didn't look any better dancing to purple or to red. However, quiet and meek, I remained silent. I didn't say anything or confront them.

Before the mean girls in dance class, it seems that I was a "mean girl" too, for one part of second grade. On one of my quarter report cards, Ms. Halford gave me an S-minus in courtesy. I was reamed by Mom and Dad for this happening and felt so sorry about how I had treated another classmate that thankfully I was jolted out of that mean-girl behavior. However, while I was back to being nice, I still wasn't standing up for myself or standing up to my classmates in play situations.

The turning point for my mind-set was soccer. I started playing when I was nine years old because American Youth Soccer Organization (AYSO) was the thing to do. It took me a few years, but every year I played, I got better and better. In turn, that invigorated me. I eventually became an outstanding player, scoring many goals and standing out on defense too. I realized I excelled as an athlete. I also found out I was fiercely competitive: I didn't just want to play; I wanted to win. Being assertive and aggressive on the soccer field is what you needed to do if you wanted to win. And I wanted to win every game.

My body was allowing me to achieve, giving me a newfound confidence. I liked how I felt in my body as I continued to score more goals and reach new goals. Soccer. Volleyball. Basketball. Soccer MVP, volleyball starter, basketball starter at point guard, fierce athlete, student council, drama, choir, talent shows, straight-A student. I was a classic overachiever.

A teenager now, all I wanted to do for my thirteenth birthday was to wear my paint-splattered sweatshirt with the neck cut out and go see the movie *Flashdance*. So, Mom and Dad took two of my best girlfriends and me, only thinking the film was a "dance" movie, not knowing it was an R-rated movie with some serious sexy sex. In the film, Jennifer Beals plays Alex, an eighteen-year-old who is a welder by day and a go-go dancer by night. With dreams of being a ballet star, she falls in love with the Porsche-driving boss of the construction company she works for. The hot and heavy steel mill scene with Alex and Nick was the first time I saw a man put his hand under a woman's shirt—my first visual cue that a woman's breasts were a part of sex. Dad instantly blurted out a loud "Oy!" and stomped out to the lobby, mortified that he had brought my friends and me to see this movie. For the longest time, Mom thought the *Flashdance* song lyrics "Take your passion and make it happen" were "Take your pants off and make it happen."

At fifteen, I had an older boyfriend who made my body feel new things, things like I'd seen in the *Flashdance* movie. However, I also had a feeling that I was way too young—both emotionally and physically—to be having sex and that it was not the right time for me to be going all the way. I was not ready for sex. I did not want it to happen, so it didn't happen. He broke up with me.

I was overachieving in high school, running from sports practice to drama rehearsal. I was president of my high school sophomore class. I had friends. However, a feeling inside me became overwhelming and told me my current high school wasn't the place for me. I just had a profound sense that it was in my best interests to go to the other high school in the area where I was not zoned. I had no hesitation. However, I was going to have to plead my case with Mom and Dad. It took a bit of courage to talk to them, but I did, and it worked. I attended junior and senior year at the other high school.

College allowed me ultimate freedom for the first time. While I could have played soccer in college, I dropped the sport cold turkey, frustrated, because there were no opportunities for women in soccer beyond college back then. I saw no point in continuing something when I could not have a career doing it. Away from home on my own, I was in a whole new environment without soccer. Along with gaining the "freshman fifteen," I gained a new sense of awareness of my body. It was my year of exploration and my year of dating many different boys.

In charge of my day-to-day life, I realized it was I who was in control of my own body, my destiny. No parents were there to tell me what to do. I was on an open field, trying out new moves and new things and experimenting with these new sexual feelings. I was getting in touch with what made me feel good, feel happy, feel womanly. I was in control, and it felt powerful—exactly how I wanted to be feeling.

By sophomore year of college, my feelings also told me not to be a complete idiot and to get it together. No more freshman craziness. I was over it anyway. It was now time to get serious about my future, so I focused on school. It was important to me that I look to my future, so by junior year I got an internship in the entertainment industry, I had one serious boyfriend, and I bailed out of most college-related social activities.

I was getting a sense of who I was in the world, and my feelings were continuing to guide me.

PART II
LILIES

CHAPTER

4

Gilda and Norene

Journalists were hounding the hospital trying to find out what had happened to Gilda Radner. Gene Wilder had to change her name on all the medical records, "Lily Herman" was what he came up with—Lily, for what they had dreamt of naming a daughter, and Herman, for her father's name.[1]

It was at the end of my junior year of college that I experienced a feeling when Gilda Radner died. It was May 20, 1989, nine days before my twentieth birthday. Flashdance sweatshirts, leg warmers, totally tubular lingo, and poofy hair were coming to an end, and I found myself unusually jolted by Radner's death. Even in my still somewhat naive, immortal teenage mind, I couldn't shake the feeling of the tragedy. It was horrifying to me that Radner had died so young. This "ovarian cancer" she'd died from seemed to be a particularly cruel disease.

I knew Gilda Radner from *Saturday Night Live* and enjoyed her character Roseanne Roseannadanna, the ornery Italian news commentator widely known for her catchphrase "It's always something!" which ended up being the title of Radner's memoir.

Radner was married to *Willy Wonka & the Chocolate Factory* and *Blazing Saddles* star Gene Wilder. Sometime in 1986, Radner started experiencing fatigue and sharp pain in her upper thighs.

Wilder reported, "Well, the doctors said, 'She's very excitable, a little neurotic, and it will go away.' Then ten months later she was given a blow, stage IV ovarian cancer."[2]

Gilda started to bloat so much that her belly stuck out like a balloon. When she first heard the phrase ovarian cancer on October 21, 1986, Radner cried, but then she turned to Wilder and said, "Thank God, finally someone believes me!" Gilda suffered extreme physical and emotional pain during chemotherapy and radiotherapy treatment. Wilder reported, "When I left that night, the doctor took me outside. I never told her this, but he said, 'She doesn't have much chance.' They operated 36 hours later and found a grapefruit-sized tumor."[3]

While I didn't personally know Gilda, I did know Norene. Norene was my mom's best friend and the first person I'd known personally who had a cancer diagnosis, in this case, breast cancer. Norene stood out not because of her natural beauty or her utterly groovy permed seventies-styled wig she wore to cover up her hair loss resulting from chemotherapy but because of her effervescent spirit, her smile, and her great laugh. More than that, Mom and Norene shared the same very down-to-earth authentic vibe and a very similar ornery, witty sense of humor; this was clear to me even at seven years old. Forever etched in my mind is a picture of Norene joyfully dancing with her husband, Skip, at my brother's bar mitzvah. They were a thirty-something couple very much in love. And as Norene danced, she filled the room with a lightness that did not show the gloom of her prognosis in any way. From the happy picture, one would never guess that Norene would succumb to breast cancer at age forty. Fourteen years later, her husband, Skip, would commit suicide. He never got over losing Norene.

I was only ten when my mom was diagnosed with breast cancer. The first ten years of my life were perfect. I genuinely believe that it was those years that shaped the rest of my life. As for my parents, they had a great relationship— loving, playful. The five years postdiagnosis were riddled with treatment, and our once perfect life was now the fight of a lifetime. My dad was unbelievable during those years and incredibly supportive toward my mom until she took her last breath on October 6, 1978. My grandmother also played a major role in that time. She was at our house every day of the five years. My mom was my dad's rudder. I believe she grounded him and kept him balanced. After she died, everything fell apart.

—Valerie, Norene's daughter

Over the years I started hearing more stories of people diagnosed with cancer beyond Gilda and Norene—and with all different types of cancer. At first, it was the "daughter of So-and-So," the "son-in-law of my parents' friends," or "So-and-So's mom (or dad)." As time went on, the names became recognizable: Helen, the rabbi's wife; my neighbor Maggie; my husband's work colleague Kristin. Some of these people survived their cancer diagnosis, and some did not. It seemed that every year there were more names of people I knew who were diagnosed. It appeared the proximity of cancer was creeping closer and closer.

CHAPTER

—— 5 ——

Sista

I feel the earth move under my feet
I feel the sky tumbling down.[1]
—Carole King

Track 7, "It's Over," from Boz Scaggs's new album *Silk Degrees*, would bounce off the turntable and off the stark white walls of Sista's bedroom, vibrating up through her groovy grass-green carpet, eventually landing on her cozy queen-size mattress, where I would sit. Awestruck with admiration, I watched as Sista repeated her pom-pom routines over and over, always flawlessly.

Even though I loved the pom-poms, my favorite of Sista's routines was one that didn't include any music; it was a cheer. "S-C-O-R-E, *score! Score!*" Arms up, cross right arm over left in a circle, then right arm to left knee and left knee up! Again. "S-C-O-R-E, *score! Score!*"

I never understood how Sista's perfectly styled feathered hair would always fall right back into place after she whipped her head around and around. I could watch her for hours. However, she would end up kicking me out of her room at some point—never meanly though. She was always very poised and straightforward.

Jan—"Sista," as I call her—is the oldest of my siblings and precisely nine years older than me, so in 1976 when she was sixteen, choreographing these pom-pom routines, I was only seven years old, still hopscotching on the playground.

Sporting clogs, bell-bottoms, and that feathered hair, Sista was going to high school parking lot parties, football games, and proms. Me, I was digging up slugs and bugs, collecting Bonne Bell Lip Smackers, and hoping my perfect memory of my multiplication tables would earn me a trip to the local Baskin-Robbins ice cream store for a double scoop of peanut butter chocolate and chocolate chip ice cream.

An especially good time for us hanging out in her room would be listening to either Boz Scaggs or one of her funkadelic eight-track tapes, such as Parliament or the Commodores. Sometimes before bed, she would let me hop into a bathtub with her to finish our night of girly fun.

As a seven-year-old, I looked at Sista and wondered about our similar, yet very different, bodies.

Okay, why are Sista's boobs bigger? Why does she have hair down there?

Sista, knowing I was looking and wondering, one time said, "One day you will grow up and look like this too." My jaw clenching and my eyes popping out simultaneously, I thought, *We-e-e-e ird. Very weird.*

A year later when I was eight, an entirely creepy set of circumstances brought Sista and me even closer. She became a huge source of strength and comfort for me. As a third grader, I was part tomboy, part Hello Kitty—independent and creative, yet innocent and naive too. Living on the hedge above our driveway were Maca and Tica, my two imaginary friends, with whom I would still visit and to whom I would talk on a regular basis.

My hands cupped my face, and my elbows dug into the shag carpet, as Rodge, Rerun, Dee, and Dwayne were cracking me up one night on one of my favorite television shows, *What's Happening!* At a commercial break, I zoned out and looked up, seeing a figure standing behind our large oak tree outside the window. The figure was waving something at me and laughing.

Someone had robbed our house while Mom, Sista, and I were home. Only as an adult did I come to realize that it was money this person was waving at me, money he or she had stolen from inside our house. The night of the robbery, initially no one believed that I had seen a person behind the oak tree. However, when Dad and my brothers returned home and bedroom doors were opened and money found missing, I was validated. Unfortunately, I was also completely freaked out and became a terrified eight-year-old. This experience haunted me for the majority of my younger years.

Sista tucked me into her daisy flower sheets that night to get some rest. Dad woke me up at one in the morning for the police to question me, my pink kitty-cat nightgown draping over my toes as he carried me downstairs. After that night, I slept with Sista in her bed on and off for two years. She became my ultimate source of comfort. She became my method of feeling safe.

Repeatedly, Sista would ask me at bedtime, "Amers"—her nickname for me—"will you please scratch my back? Please, will you scraaaatch? C'monnnn, pleeeeasse scratch my back. You scratch me first, and I promise I will scratch yours right after."

I didn't mind scratching her back at all, except that every time she would ask me to scratch, she would fall asleep as if on cue after ten minutes. That is, she would fall asleep without reciprocating the back-scratching.

Inevitably, the next night Sista would say with her sweet, tired eyes, "Amers, scraaaatch. C'mon, Amers, pleeeease scratch my back. I promise I will scratch yours right after." So I would scratch, and on cue Sista would fall asleep! Over and over, again and again, she did not reciprocate the back-scratching! She would fall asleep every time.

Honestly, when she fell asleep, it didn't bug me that much. Ultimately, I just wanted to feel secure, be cozy, and sleep next to Sista. I loved her very much and looked up to her in so many ways, so I didn't care that she would fall asleep on me without back-scratching reciprocation.

Since Sista was a very busy high schooler, I thought she just must be really, really, really tired.

It must take a lot of energy to do those cheers and pom-pom routines.

Sista went off to college at UCLA. I grew up and went off to college at USC. We were close—and then we would have our differences. We would be close, and then we would have our differences—back and forth, back and forth.

We were very different in both personality and physique. Sista, a true fashionista, was striking, put together, and almost six feet tall in her Jimmy Choos, whereas I always preferred comfort over fashion and stood a healthy five foot three in my Chuck Taylors. Our mannerisms and sense of humor, however, remained very, very similar. By the time I was thirty-one and about to get married in 2000, things had balanced out. Sista and I were now adult peers and downright indestructible.

She was my Sista and the number one most important person to me next to my husband, Jon, and my kids, Brooke and Ben. So when Sista called me in the summer of 2008, I immediately cringed with worry. She explained she was having what she thought were some digestive issues. Being in the fashion industry, Sista traveled regularly to New York and Los Angeles. She would fly somewhere, spend the week working, and go out to fabulous dinners at night. Sista thought maybe her frenzied schedule was the culprit—always on the fly, running around, not eating regularly, drinking too much wine. When she called me a few days later, she told me she sensed it was something more; her belly was becoming increasingly bloated, and it felt as if more was wrong than just stomach issues.

Bloated.

I heard Sista say that word, and I got a sick feeling inside. I had just read an article the week before stating that stomach bloating and distention could be a sign of ovarian cancer.

Gilda Radner immediately popped into my head. *OMG, Gilda Radner.*

It had been over a year since Sista had seen her ob-gyn. "Get your butt to the doctor!" I told her.

Sista called me on a Sunday morning while I was at a bagel shop having a family breakfast with Jon and the kids. I had been waiting for her call, so I picked up the phone. I could tell by the sound of her voice that it was bad news.

"They found a mass," Sista said. "It could or could not be cancer."

Karate-kicked right in my gut, I could not speak.

She continued, "My CA-125 was 200."

CA-125, I thought to myself. *What the heck is that?*

"What is that?" I asked. Little did I know at that point that CA-125 would soon become an all too familiar unfortunate new term in my vocabulary.

"The CA-125 is inconclusive. It's a blood marker. It could be Meigs' disease—a benign condition usually affecting the right ovary," Sista said very matter-of-factly.

Tears flooded over my tinted moisturizer, tasting salty on my lips. I got up quickly, walked to a corner of the shop near a trash can, and crouched down, not wanting Brooke and Ben to see my welled-up face. Jon saw me hiding and crying.

For the next week, I was on Google searching and researching, honestly optimistic that it could be a benign condition.

Over the next few weeks, my forty-eight-year-old Sista became increasingly bloated and distended. All the while, she was orchestrating a book release party for Dad. Sista not only continued to plan Dad's party but also ultimately attended it in her flowing designer dress, no one aware that underneath she looked six months pregnant because of the bloating and distention. That evening would be her last outing until she underwent surgery in the middle of September 2008.

I quickly mapped out care for Brooke and Ben so it would coordinate with Jon's work schedule and availability; I flew to California to be with Sista for twelve days.

I had the feeling that this was going to be the hardest twelve days of my life to date. It was clear that I must prepare. When Mom reflects back on that time, she says to me time and again, "Thank God you were there, Amy. You were a brick of strength."

Confession time. Yes, yes, Mom, I was. I *was* a brick of strength. I was a great big prepared Xanax brick of strength. One milligram of Xanax a day—starting with the one milligram I took the minute I got on the plane to fly out to the Bay Area, and including the one milligram I took every day I was out there. I was a mess. I *had* to have that Xanax—I knew I had to channel my inner superhero and be Wonder Woman–tough. Sista needed me to be, and my parents were going to need me to be too. Inside I was falling apart. This was my Sista. I did what I had to do to remain strong; I couldn't lose it. *Sista needed me.*

Sista had to wait a few weeks for her surgery date. Even if one has a connection at the hospital, it can still take time for surgery to be scheduled. So I stayed with her at her place.

While I was there, Sista's pain gradually got worse. The fluid (ascites) kept building up in her belly, so we had to go back two times to the hospital to get her drained. Each time we went, the nurse drained several liters out of her, but through it, Sista and I still managed to keep a sense of humor. We would go for her fluid removal, which was called a "paracentesis," and then we would walk to Perry's Restaurant afterward to get a bite to eat. Goofily, arm in arm, we would stroll, skip, and giggle. "We're going from 'pari' to Perry's," we'd joke, both of us finally succumbing to a complete outburst of laughter.

Unfortunately, our laughter didn't last very long.

Sista was having a terrible day; she was in excruciating, debilitating pain on the floor, at the top of her stairs, unable to move. There is nothing like having to watch someone you love have intolerable, insufferable pain. I call it death pain.

I yelled loudly in my head, *Make it stop, please!*

I felt helpless. Sista's complete physical agony became the most intense emotional agony I had ever felt in my life. *With each of her moans, I saw Sista's face morph into Gilda's face as well as our grandmother Lillian's face. Whoa.*

I kept "yelling" out in my head, *This pain! Please make her pain stop. Make it stop!*

I drove ferociously to the hospital to get her more Percocet, all the while thinking about that scene from *Terms of Endearment* where Shirley MacLaine's character runs up to the nurse's desk and screams, "Give my daughter her medicine!"

I got the Percocet for Sista and then drove like a madwoman back to her house. She took the Percocet.

It did nothing.

Frantically, I called up Sista's doctor's office and demanded they admit her to the hospital. Emotional, but also assertive and firm, I cried out, "Her pain is not being managed!" *Something* took over my body that wouldn't take no for an answer. "I'm bringing her in!" I declared. It was my Shirley MacLaine moment.

Sista was admitted to the hospital and stayed there until her surgery a few days later. We were all there the day of her surgery— Mom, Dad, my two brothers, and me. In the surgical waiting room, anesthetized with Xanax, I zoned out; each of their voices sounded like Charlie Brown's teacher.

Sista's surgeon, a gynecological oncologist, came out after four hours and delicately talked to us, this very lost herd of deer in headlights. We all scanned the surgeon's face to see what the road ahead would look like for all of us. "It is cancer," the surgeon said, "a mass on her ovary the size of a grapefruit. We did a complete hysterectomy plus took part of her omentum."

Ba-ba-boom! A big rig hit something on the dark road. One doe and one buck down! There go my parents. Next truck is coming. "Here is the picture of her insides." Sista's surgeon calmly pointed. "See the grapefruit?" *Swerve, smash!* Two more roadkills; my two brother bucks lay there in lifeless shells.

Sista's surgeon tried to revive all of us with some positive news. "Well, the cancer looked to be contained and lower staging, but we will have to wait for final pathology."

I was waiting for overdrive to hit the last remaining Bambi: me. I was waiting. Truck, car, anything? Anything on the road ahead to knock me down?

There was nothing.

Xanax and coffee were keeping my hind legs afloat. My last sip of coffee was cold, but I'd gulped it down anyway, totally unfazed by the nasty chalky hospital creamer that had accumulated on the bottom of the Styrofoam cup. As I sat in my caffeinated numbness, all I could think about was Gilda Radner. Gilda also had a tumor the size of a grapefruit. I knew that there were breast cancer survivors, but I had not heard of an ovarian cancer survivor.

CHAPTER

6

Kristin

"Surprise!" everyone happily shouted as Jon walked into the lunch and the Beatles tribute band played "Today Is Your Birthday."

I got him. Jon was in complete shock.

Before Sista's ovarian cancer diagnosis and surgery back in May, I had started planning a fortieth surprise birthday party for Jon's September birthday. How I'd managed to keep Jon's party even happening, plus keep it a secret from him, is beyond me.

I was singularly focused on Sista and being held together by a mere thread. When I returned to Florida, Dad, unexpectedly, had to undergo emergency triple bypass heart surgery. It was all too much. I was still going forward with Jon's party, but truthfully it was the last thing on my mind.

Was it the Xanax holding me together? Perhaps. I do know my anally retentive preorganization for the party in May and June had paid off. However, I felt my sanity running on fumes. I was not all there, but *something kept me going*. Initially, I was going to have Jon's fortieth be a blowout of epic proportion, but with everything happening with Sista, I ended up cutting the guest list way down to include only Jon's closest colleagues, his closest friends, and our family.

The feeling was, *Keep things simple; you need your strength.* Mom and Dad were supposed to fly out for the party, but because of Dad's surgery, clearly they weren't coming.

With all that was going on with Dad and Sista, Jon could not believe I had pulled off this surprise party. His reaction was priceless, and he was beyond thrilled with all who were there for him to help celebrate, especially our dear friend and his former coanchor Kristin Hoke Cecere and her adorable, not quite one-year-old daughter Bella.

Jon had coanchored the five o'clock morning show with Kristin. He had worked as a reporter for the local ABC station here in West Palm Beach starting in 1998, and in January of 2002 he had switched over to working with Kristin.

Initially unsure if he wanted to work the early shift, Jon called Kristin, and Kristin urged him, "C'mon, Jon, just do it. Let's have fun." So, Jon did it—and continued anchoring with Kristin through the fall of 2003. Their on-set chemistry was undeniable. It's still fun to watch their old news stories that can be found online.

> While most of America is sleeping, the morning television news anchor is already at work. It is his or her job to welcome thousands of people into each day gently. It requires a particular kind of congeniality; an honest face, a steady voice, a comforting presence that says, "I'm here to get you up to date on what's happening in your world." Working with Kristin for nearly two years on that shift at WPBF, I marveled at her ability to be that person, not just at work but also in life.

Her demeanor is so perfectly suited for the job. It's tough to shake the cobwebs with 2:30 a.m. wake-up calls, but Kristin never came into that shift without a smile on her face. Always sharp as a tack, she could recall background on any story, local or national, that needed added context.

I remember when we took our morning show on the road. Good Morning America was broadcasting in Miami Beach, so as an ABC affiliate from West Palm Beach, our station took our crew to the sand. At the time, the GMA anchors were Diane Sawyer and Charles Gibson. Always able to relate to anyone, Kristin had no problem talking to two of the biggest names in the game!

—Jon Shainman

I was a busy new mom when Jon and Kristin started anchoring together, so I didn't meet Kristin until she and Jon had been working side by side for about a year. Kristin and I first met in the news station parking lot.

A woman in red was approaching in an orangey, tomato-red suit. Immediately I thought, *Wow, who the hell looks good in that color?* Then I answered myself: *OMG, she does. Um, wow, she has incredible legs! Okay, what a figure. This gal is sincerely one hot tamale.*

She got closer to me, and I saw her lightly tanned skin and exceedingly beautiful face. *So, this dazzling woman is whom my husband has been hanging out with on the news set in the middle of the night and early morning? Argh!* I grunt as I adjust my baseball cap and cower. *Why do I suddenly feel as if I need a considerable amount of self tanner, a new wardrobe, and two personal trainers?* There was no time for contemplation or self-pity as outstretched arms and an electric white smile completely enveloped me.

"Hiiiiii! *Amy!*" Kristin's enthusiasm and down-to-earth joy were multiple shades brighter than her tomato-red suit.

"Kristin!" I answered, hugging her back. But inside I felt mortified because of the rumpled sweatpants mom look that I was sporting.

Oh, just to hate her would have been so much easier. But of course, I immediately loved her. I couldn't help but love her. Everything about her was genuine, the real deal, no pretense or facade. She was merely herself: Kristin.

I joked, trying to break the ice. "So *you're* the one hanging out with my husband in the middle of the night!" Instantaneously, we both burst out laughing. "I have wanted to meet you for a long time," I said.

With the same unbridled enthusiasm she'd used when she greeted me, she replied, "Me too!" Then the gorgeous natural beauty channeled a fun Dolly Parton–like attitude and twang. "Ya know, I just *luuuv* your husband!"

"Well, then." I smiled. "We have something in common. I do too."

We became friends.

Kristin: kind, funny, personable, and gorgeous.

Upon seeing Kristin at Jon's fortieth birthday party, I also decided she was one of two people on the planet who looked absolutely, downright *stunning* with absolutely no hair. There was Sinead O'Connor in the 1980s, and then there was Kristin Hoke.

Even with her lack of hair, the result of the chemotherapy due to a recurrence of breast cancer, Kristin still looked unbelievable—one of those women who could wear a garbage bag and look fabulous, one of those women who roll out of bed looking great. Plus she was warm, friendly, and so darn likable too—Meg Ryan in *When Harry Met Sally*, quirky and down-to-earth, and with a hefty dose of Natalie Portman sex appeal and natural beauty. Kristin, initially diagnosed with an early stage cancer in the left breast in 2004, underwent treatment—with breast conservation—including lumpectomy and sentinel lymph node biopsy. The breast cancer was triple-negative and poorly differentiated, which is a more aggressive type of breast cancer.

> Kristin and I met at Channel 25. I was the morning news floor director. We became friends first, for about a year. She was married to her first husband then. Right after she got separated is when things started. She initiated. We started going to lunch. We kept it kind of private. We went to Costa Rica and stayed at that little Holiday Inn—I'd surf and we'd go to dinner on the beach. We had a blast. I thought she was an amazing and beautiful woman. We got married in 2004. It was shortly after we were married in 2004 when she was first diagnosed with breast cancer. I came home one day, and Kristin let me touch her breast. The lump was in her left breast.
>
> —Eric Cecere

Kristin, a vibrant personality, was initially painfully shy as a kid. It wasn't that she didn't have anything to say; it was just that she couldn't get a word in edgewise. She was the youngest of five, with two brothers and two sisters. She had a great childhood in Michigan and was extremely close to her mom. In fifth grade, Kristin auditioned and landed the role of Brigitta in *The Sound of Music*. Dozens of parts that followed drew her out of her shell. It was her love of performing that led her to broadcasting.

Kristin studied at the University of Michigan vocational school for reporting. Initially she was interested in a big market, either

Chicago or Detroit. Before working in West Palm Beach, Kristin worked in Fresno, and before that she was fired from her first job in Knoxville, Tennessee, for saying on air that the guest chef made a meatball that looked like a turd.

Kristin devoted herself to cancer research and finding a cure. She used her platform as a news anchor and reporter to document her breast cancer and her experience.

> KRISTIN. I show the really dark moments, the shaving of my head, going through surgeries, because I don't ever want someone to think that it's not hard. It's difficult.

> ERIC. As traumatizing as the cancer diagnosis was, I think she was even more devastated by the possibility she would not be able to have a child.

> KRISTIN. My lifelong dream was to become a mother. There was nothing I wanted more. Since seventh grade, I'd been around babies. I was an aunt to ten nieces and nephews. Family is everything.

> ERIC. I remember sitting in Dr. Rimmer's office and [Kristin] crying because all she wanted was to have a child. Having a child is all she cared about. Dr. Rimmer discussed the cell definition structure of her cancer. Kristin had a lumpectomy, and Dr. Rimmer felt like he got it all. She shaved her head. After Kristin's lumpectomy, radiation, and chemotherapy, Dr. Rimmer suggested she have a double mastectomy. But

Kristin wanted to be able to breastfeed. We got the go ahead to try for a baby a year and a half after treatment. We got pregnant with Bella quickly.

KRISTIN. Bella was my little miracle. What shaped my own childhood was time outdoors, camping, fishing, swimming, and boating. I'd canoe and fish on the Treasure Coast in Jensen Beach, Florida. My father and uncle could be described as fishing fanatics. They had an utter love of creatures in the ocean.

I did more than ten years of ballet and jazz and was a cheerleader three years in a row, eventually becoming cheerleading captain to seventeen men and women! Before the Detroit Lions had cheerleaders, my squad would cheer at their games. I guess it was just in my blood; my mom was also a cheerleader. I think Bella will be lucky if she discovers dance, theater, or the great outdoors. Those things helped me become the person I am.

Emails between Me, Jon, and Kristin

FALL 2008

From: Kristin Hoke Cecere
Sent: October 3, 2008
To: Amy Byer Shainman

Amy and Jon,

I just wanted to tell you what a great time I had at your party.
I haven't laughed like that in a while. Bella slept for four hours
that afternoon; she was tuckered out!

But I was mainly writing to see how you are doing, Amy. I have
had you constantly on my mind. Just know I will be praying for
your dad and sister. I would be happy to share anything I know
about both subjects [surgery and cancer], only if you feel like
talking.

Hang in there. You can get through tough times with love and
prayer. Family is everything.

Kristin

• • •

From: Amy Byer Shainman
Sent: October 6, 2008
To: Kristin Hoke Cecere

Hi, Kristin,
Thanks for the email!
My dad is finally out of ICU—had a few setbacks. He's eighty-one, so the recovery is going to be slow and long.
He's swearing and irritated, so I take that as a good sign!
My sister starts her chemo on the fifteenth. Her final diagnosis was ovarian cancer stage IC (very good—we got lucky) and uterine cancer stage IA (no treatment needed—it is a moot point now since she had the total hysterectomy).
I feel we are getting very lucky on all of this.
Thank you for your continued good thoughts and prayers.
I'm so happy you and Bella had such a good time.
Jon was thrilled with the day.
How are your Boston trips/treatments going? You are always on our minds as well. Let us know what you need. That Bella is just delicious, and I still would love to watch her anytime.

:) Amy

• • •

From: Kristin Hoke Cecere
Sent: October 13, 2008
To: Amy Byer Shainman

That is great news about [your] dad and sister. Dad's spunk will go a long way—really. Being pissed is a good rallying position!

With any reproductive cancers, always ask about connecting tubes. For instance, women will take out their ovaries and not their fallopian tubes leading up to the ovaries and then have issues there later. (Got to get it all.) Just make sure they do a really good exam of all the surrounding areas.

The IC is very good. I have heard good solid outcomes out of that stage—very good. I swear, Amy—some of the most impressive new drugs going on the market in the next six to twelve months are for ovarian. The clinical drug I am on was first proven for ovarian (people who had no chance to live at all . . . alive years later), so even though it's one of the scariest cancers, it is treatable. You should also know that I plan to take out my ovaries in about a year because it is a 99.8 percent cure for folks like me. (I am twenty times greater at risk because of the breast cancer gene.)

I am so glad you wrote back. My prayers to you guys. You are so strong and will be such a great force in your loved ones' recoveries.

My surgery went really well. I am headed back to work Tuesday (tomorrow!). Crazy, huh? Talk about modern medicine! Brain surgery!
Eric said now I can really claim that I have a screw loose to people! I laughed and said, "Honey I had a screw loose when I married ya!" Ha-ha!
Love you. Hang in there.
And please ask me anything along the way; I can always find out from comoonel

Kristin

• • •

From: Kristin Hoke Cecere
Sent: December 11, 2008
To: Jon Shainman

How are you guys doing?

The holidays can be so rough with health challenges.
Give me an update. And more importantly, have you heard anything about your contract and gig?
Selfishly, I would love to have you back on mornings, even though it sucks hours-wise.
Great family-wise.
I don't know if that is even an option being discussed.
Love you. I hope it all settles out real soon.

Kristin

• • •

From: Jon Shainman
Sent: December 15, 2008,
To: Kristin Hoke Cecere

Hey yourself. All is okay with us. My sister-in-law is still under-going chemo. She's got a few more treatments—should be done in February/March. Amy and kids heading out there this weekend. I'll head out after Xmas Day for a week.

As for me here, we shall see. An a.m. reunion would take some serious body clock readjusting!

Jon

• • •

From: Kristin Hoke Cecere
Sent: December 17, 2008,
To: Jon Shainman

If Amy needs any advice on her sister dealing with chemo, she can always call or write.

But pass this onto her:

For sour stomach, try Carafate liquid. It has been around forever and costs about five bucks with a prescription. (It is a liquid, so you have instant relief, and it doesn't compete with pills that are dissolving. I think it is much better than Pepcid, Prilosec, etc.) She should also try a natural supplement for added intestinal bacteria (chemo kills these in the intestines). Get it at Nutrition Smart for about ten bucks. You can buy active cultures or off-the-shelf. I say active ones. The helper at the store can point her in the right direction. Take one to two Colace pills each day—that is just the ingredient that gets things moving. There is nothing else in it. Walgreens or CVS would have it. Also, Ativan can help enormously the day of chemo to mellow you out.

And most of all, do not deal with pain. Have her ask the oncologists to [do the following]:

1. Tell her which pain "family" they are using for her (Tylenol, Percocet, etc.). I hate OxyContin, and they often prescribe that without thinking. There are other drug families that work entirely different.
2. Prescribe the smallest dosage. I go for 1 mg because I like to have control over how many 1 mg pills I take and how often. They are not used to healthy, fit women. (A perfect example: my doctor prescribed me 10 mg a day of heavy steroids. I said no. And the correct amount for my body is more like two a day of 1 mg.)

I hope this helps, honey.
Just forward it to Amy at home.

Love you both!
Kristin

• • •

PART III
SUNLIGHT AND SHADE

CHAPTER

—— 7 ——

Hail Mary!

*In 1990, Mary Claire King demonstrated that a
single gene on chromosome 17q21 (which she named
BRCA1) was responsible for breast and ovarian
cancer in many families.*[1]

Sista had two separate primary cancers. Her final pathology revealed stage IC ovarian cancer and also indicated stage IA uterine cancer. "In stage IA uterine cancer, cancer is in the endometrium only or less than halfway through the myometrium (the muscle layer of the uterus)."[2] *How did we get so lucky with Sista?* Her ovarian cancer was stage IC? I could not believe it. No one could believe it—especially with the grapefruit-sized ovarian tumor. Gilda Radner also had a grapefruit-sized ovarian tumor. Gilda's ovarian cancer was stage IV. How was Sista's grapefruit-sized tumor only stage IC?

> Early-stage ovarian cancer rarely causes any symptoms. Advanced-stage ovarian cancer may cause few and nonspecific symptoms that

are often mistaken for more common benign
conditions, such as constipation or irritable
bowel. Ovarian cancer often goes undetected
until it has spread within the pelvis and abdomen. At this late stage, ovarian cancer is
more difficult to treat and is frequently fatal.
Early-stage ovarian cancer, in which the disease
is confined to the ovary, is more likely to be
treated successfully.[3]

Sista's surgeon said that her tumor was "contained" but recommended she undergo six rounds of chemotherapy to make sure
all of her cancer was gone.

I had a massive amount of guilt about not being able to be
there for Sista for her chemo sessions. However, my feelings told
me that my young kids needed me at home. *My family needed me
more now.*

I think Sista knows I would have done almost anything
to be able to "scratch her back" while she underwent chemo.
Thankfully, Megan, Sista's dearest friend since age fourteen, was
available to stay with Sista for two months and go with her to
chemo sessions.

Sista will officially hate the next paragraph.

Sista. She is seriously the hottest, most fashionable cancer
patient. Hair or no hair, she always makes a statement when she
walks into a room. Cancer or no cancer, she has the most fantastic
wardrobe and sense of style. She wore YSL (Yves Saint Laurent)
high heels to her chemo sessions. At forty-eight years old, while
enduring chemotherapy, she was asked by two separate people if
she was a model.

Being the fashionista that she is, losing her hair was hard for
Sista. So she took it upon herself to invest in fifteen (yes, fifteen)
fabulous wigs—and then name them, of course. There was the

caramel-colored "Lindsay Lohan," which was cute, but I was partial to blonde "Hannah Montana." Brooke and Ben loved to try on "Hannah," and we all agreed that Ben looked unusually fabulous in that one! We took a lot of pictures and laughed. The kids had fun but thought it was kinda weird that Auntie Jan's medicine made her hair fall out. Still, they both said, "The wigs are kinda cool."

In early 2009 I had seen a television commercial and also a pamphlet in my ob-gyn's office about something called *BRCA* analysis and something to do with ovarian cancer in one's family. I thought maybe I should get that testing done. Kristin had also mentioned something about the breast cancer gene, although I didn't ask her about it.

Then in March 2009 I had unexplained abdominal pain. Was I a hypochondriac? With Sista's medical history, I was freaking out. What was the pain? I asked my ob-gyn for a CT scan.

Barium drink down; CT scan clear; relief!

Jon ended up turning the tables on me in May and surprised me for my fortieth birthday. He got me back good with a great surprise trip to Las Vegas. Even though Sista had just finished a round of chemo, she hopped on a plane to Vegas! The nonstop jingle of the slot machines couldn't even compare to my screams, which must still be echoing somewhere at that casino!

Note: That was the best birthday ever.

Sista finished with chemo, and life was slowly getting back to normal for her and everyone else in our family. There happened to be an ovarian cancer conference in October of 2009, and Sista decided she would go. Sista just had a gut feeling, *something telling her she should go* to get more knowledge.

> About one year after my surgery, I decided
> to attend an ovarian cancer conference. My

takeaway from that conference was that I should get genetic testing ASAP.

Why?

The reasons are as follows:

- I am of Ashkenazi Jewish descent.
- I had two primary cancers at the same time (uterine cancer and ovarian cancer).
- I was under fifty years old.
- There was a family history of breast cancer on my dad's side of the family (yes, the paternal side matters!).

So, I made an appointment with the genetic counselor at the hospital where I was treated. After taking down my entire family history, the genetic counselor said she would present it to the hospital board to get approval for the genetic testing to be covered by my insurance. In 2009, it seemed I had enough medically going on to warrant the genetic testing, but she said that I would probably be "negative."

When I went back to the genetic counselor for my genetic testing results, she was very apologetic for suggesting to me that I was most likely negative.

It turned out that I was *BRCA1* positive. All that I could think about was my sister, Amy. Then, the genetic counselor informed me that *all* of my siblings needed to be tested, not just my sister but also my brothers.

—Jan Byer (Sista)

Sista's take-home message from the ovarian cancer conference was "Get genetic testing! Get *BRCA* testing." It was *that* test—the test in the pamphlet that I had seen in my ob-gyn's office.

CHAPTER

8

Me

Epiphany. The puzzle pieces began to form a picture. Sista had a genetic mutation—a *BRCA1* genetic mutation. We learned that having a *BRCA1* or *BRCA2* gene mutation significantly increases a woman's risk of breast and ovarian cancer. We learned about this from the ovarian cancer conference, and subsequently we learned more from Sista's genetic counselor. I asked Ellen Matloff, MS, CGC, the President and CEO of My Gene Counsel, and the founder and former director of the Cancer Genetic Counseling Program at Yale School of Medicine, to explain the basics of *BRCA*.

BRCA: The Basics

Every cell in our body contains 23 pairs of long, thin structures called chromosomes. We inherit one chromosome of each pair from our mother, and the other from our father. Most mutations in the BReast CAncer susceptibility genes (*BRCA*) are inherited from the mother or father, rather than representing new (or de novo) genetic changes. This means that at some point in time, the DNA of a relative changed or mutated and that genetic change has been passed down through the generations.

Our genetic information is stored on our chromosomes in tiny units called genes.

We have tens of thousands of genes that help code for everything about our bodies: from eye color to hair color to disease risks. We all have two copies of *BRCA1*, one on each of our two #17 chromosomes. A woman who inherits one mutation in *BRCA1* is at an increased risk of developing both breast and ovarian cancer, while a man who carries a *BRCA1* mutation is at an increased risk for breast and prostate cancer.

BRCA2 is located on chromosome 13, and we all have two copies of this gene. Women with one *BRCA2* mutation are at an increased risk of developing breast, ovarian, and pancreatic cancer while men who carry one *BRCA2* mutation are at an increased risk of breast, prostate, and pancreatic cancer. Many of the *BRCA* mutations can be traced back hundreds or thousands of years.[1]

—Ellen Matloff, MS, CGC, My Gene Counsel

Sista's particular gene mutation was one of the three *BRCA* genetic mutations associated with people of Ashkenazi Jewish descent. Sista seemed to be aware of there being breast cancer on Dad's side of the family. However, I wasn't aware, and Dad did not talk about it with me either. The information was all new to me and hitting our entire family and me.

That letter I'd found in Dad's junk closet about my grand-mother six years ago! *Whoa, goosebumps as I realized my grandmother Lillian had breast cancer.* She was so young when she died, only thirty-three years old. There was a family history. It was hereditary. Shivers continued through my body as I processed this and also the mammogram I'd insisted on having back in 2003 without even really knowing why.

Dad now had his epiphany of why his mom, Lillian, had died so young. It was clear by his quiet reaction and what he chose not to communicate that he carried a significant amount of guilt; he knew he'd passed a gene mutation onto his eldest daughter and possibly to his youngest one too.

All of this information was new to and very raw for our family. I just got the feeling deep in my gut that this was beyond important stuff. So, I started to write everything down in a journal. Although I didn't know what genetic testing would mean for me, I had the feeling that, whatever my genetic testing result, it was going to have a direct impact on my future. I decided I wanted to document my experience as a record not only for myself, my kids, my husband, and future generations of my family but also for others who could possibly be helped by my sharing it. Perhaps someone out there would be able to gain insight or benefit in some way from my experience.

My competitive nature and drive that had begun on the soccer field was lending itself to this medical situation. I wanted to be in control of things. I didn't want any surprises. I wanted to know as much as I could as a patient. Medically, I wanted to be able to be in the driver's seat if I could; I saw no benefit in me not knowing and not undergoing genetic testing. I wanted to win.

I saw nothing positive coming from burying my head in the sand and ignoring medical information. I thought if I had an oppor-tunity to get helpful, actionable information regarding my health, then I needed to get it. A large part of my needing to know was that

I felt a huge parental responsibility, a substantial familial obligation to follow through on getting medical information so that I could remain healthy for my kids.

I went to my ob-gyn and shared that my sister had tested positive for a *BRCA1* genetic mutation, and he referred me to a certified genetic counselor. I went to see the counselor with my sister's results in hand. The counselor spent a good hour explaining things to me.

One thing I learned while at that appointment was that insurance companies usually require a documented family history of cancer, documented gene mutation in the family, or two or more primary cancers in an individual before they will approve genetic testing. So for insurance reasons, it's ideal first to test the person affected by cancer in a family. I was comforted by the fact that this certified genetic counselor had explained everything to me in a manner I could understand.

The counselor also put the vial of my blood in the genetic testing kit right in front of me. She was insistent that there be no misstep because information from these tests is just too important. Health decisions were going to be made based on these test results. "You need to know it's your test, your blood, and your results," she said.

You know phone vibe? It's when you pick up the phone and you can instantly tell the vibe of the person on the other line. When the genetic counselor called me a few weeks later, immediately, I recognized the tone in her voice. I knew what my test result was merely by hearing her greeting of "Hi, Amy." I knew that I was positive for a *BRCA1* gene mutation, no. 5385—the same *BRCA1* gene mutation as my sister.

"I'm so sorry," said the genetic counselor.

We spoke for a bit, and then the genetic counselor referred me directly to a medical oncologist who specialized in high-risk patients. The oncologist was someone who could act as my manager, an expert in high-risk genetics who could more thoroughly advise me of my options and walk me through the next steps. Only later did I come to realize how important it was to have a clinician specializing in high-risk patients monitoring me.

I felt compelled to share my results immediately with my family and a few close friends.

• • •

From: Amy Byer Shainman
Sent: December 12, 2009
To: Family and Friends

Family and Friends:

So, here's the story.

Unfortunately, I tested positive for the *BRCA1* gene mutation 5385 (also known as no. 5382).

It's the same gene mutation Jan (Sista) has—it is one of the Ashkenazi Jewish gene mutations. This is most definitely what Dad's mom [our grandmother Lillian] had [which led to her breast cancer at such a young age], as well as Dad's aunts.

I have been advised to see a medical oncologist who specializes In genetic patients at high risk for breast and ovarian cancer. Jon and I will meet with her in the next few weeks. I may have some major decisions to make regarding my female reproductive organs. Oy.

Anyway, not to put a damper on Hanukkah or the holidays, but I thought I should fill you guys in . . .

Hey, bros, I'm going to be a pesty little sister and urge you to get your testing! If not for you, do it for your kids.

Off my soapbox now.

Love, xxxx oooo,
Amy

• • •

Even though Jon and I didn't know entirely what this genetic mutation meant for me, we did know this information was about to lead my life, our relationship, and our family down a different path.

Three years of dating long distance helped both Jon and me prepare for this new unknown situation. Trust between us was thick. Besides, I knew from how he'd handled past medical situations with me that I could count on him. He was going to be the absolute best support system. I'm not the type of person who likes someone smothering me or who wants to talk nonstop about what I am feeling. I need to research things and let them soak in on my own. Jon knew how to be there for me and support me, all without stifling me.

My comfort level with Jon allowed me to inform him not so gently, "Honey, I am going to do whatever I need to do to get myself through this next month processing all of this *BRCA* stuff, taking tests, and meeting with the medical oncologist. I am going to self-medicate any way that I need to—pop Xanax; drink heavily (okay, so I did promise not to combine the drinking with the Xanax); stuff myself with chocolate, candy, cookies, and ice cream; eat whatever I want; and do whatever I need to do. So, for the next month, honey, please just continue to support me, and please don't look at my growing ass." He obliged.

When Amy told me she was *BRCA* positive,
my initial reaction was panic. She had a *BRCA1*
gene mutation just like my colleague Kristin! I
feared the worst. But I also knew that Amy had
the same internal fortitude as Kristin and would
do whatever it took to find a solution.

—Jon Shainman

It was January 2010, and I began actively researching *BRCA*. I
was dismayed that Jessica Queller's book *Pretty Is What Changes* was
the only *BRCA* memoir I could find. Queller's book gave me and
Sista direct information on what we might be facing in the coming
months. I completely related to Jessica when she said there is your
life before you even know what *BRCA* genetic testing is and then
your life after. There is your life before you know your *BRCA* status
and then your life after. It's all-consuming.

For me, *BRCA* neurosis kicked in as I started to think about my
breasts constantly. A few times every day I would feel my breasts,
checking them for lumps. All the visuals in my life suddenly became
about my breasts. While making two eggs sunny-side up for breakfast, I looked at them in the pan and laughed with irony—boobies!
Driving in my car, I'd see a bicyclist, the two wheels on the bicycle
riding down the street—okay, boobs! Parking meter money, two
quarters—again, boobalas! Any image with two circles, and boobs
was all I could see. I felt a little "booby-trapped," pun intended.

I ordered fifteen copies of Queller's book and shipped it out to
my family and friends so they could be informed about the *BRCA*
gene mutation and understand the situation I was facing. I honestly
knew no other way to explain a *BRCA* mutation other than giving
them Queller's book.

My annual checkup would now include transvaginal ultrasound, and I would alternate every six months between mammogram with an ultrasound and a breast MRI. I knew it was essential

to get my health screenings done, but the approaching tests were causing me much anxiety and stress.

Knowing my genetic status was overwhelming. I wished I could just "check out" for several weeks while processing all this information and hook myself up to a Prozac drip. But I am a mom, and there was the matter of taking care of my kids. So checking out was not an option.

> The future of a woman carrying a *BRCA1* mutation is fundamentally changed by that knowledge—and yet it remains just as fundamentally uncertain. For some women, the genetic diagnosis is all-consuming.
> It is as if their lives and energies are spent anticipating cancer and imagining survivorship—from an illness they have not yet developed. A disturbing new word, with a distinctly Orwellian ring, has been coined to describe these women: previvors—pre-survivors . . . The prophylactic treatments—mastectomy, hormonal therapy—all entail physical and psychological anguish and carry risks in their own right.
>
> —Siddhartha Mukherjee, MD, DPhil, excerpt from his book, The Gene

CHAPTER

9

Dr. McKeen

From: Amy Byer Shainman
Sent: January 22, 2010,
To: Family and Friends

Jon and I went yesterday to the appointment with the medical oncologist who specializes in high-risk genetic patients. Her name is Dr. Elisabeth McKeen, FACP, and she is considered the guru down here. If she were not in Florida, they would have sent me to Sloan Kettering in New York. It was a very long two-hour appointment. Dr. McKeen proceeded to explain what health screenings I would need as female *BRCA1* carrier and also what my options were to reduce my cancer risk. She also gave me the results of my first breast MRI.

Options for Risk Reduction - Breasts

A) Enhanced surveillance/monitoring
B) Medication: tamoxifen (but not enough research on if it is good for hereditary cancers)

C) Prophylactic surgery: by removing breasts, it reduces your breast cancer risk by about 95 percent, and my doctor says she believes it's even more, like 98 percent, when you have a surgeon who is aggressive in removing breast tissue. Also, she says implants placed behind the muscle will push everything forward—so if you have an issue (cancer) come up in the future, it will be easier to detect.

In order to reduce ovarian cancer risk: Enhanced surveillance is unfortunately not effective at this point in time; therefore, it is highly recommended that female *BRCA1* carriers have their ovaries removed between thirty-five and forty years old, or after childbearing has been completed. My situation warranted a full hysterectomy and not just the removal of my ovaries due to Sista's diagnosis of uterine cancer. Removing ovaries before natural menopause also reduces your breast cancer risk by 50 percent.

There may be some benefit to the use of birth control pills.

Transvaginal ultrasounds aren't 100 percent effective at detecting ovarian cancer.

Melanoma: The doctor sees many *BRCA* patients with melanoma and therefore recommends an annual dermatological exam, and a formal eye exam, as melanoma can occur in the eye.

A colonoscopy at fifty.

BRCA1 in men: My doctor admits that many other doctors are not well versed in *BRCA* in men—or they don't have any knowledge about *BRCA* at all. She does see prostate cancer in *BRCA1* men (in addition to *BRCA2* men) and advises all *BRCA*-positive men to start full prostate exams by age forty.

My breast MRI: While my mammogram and mammogram ultrasound were "okay," the more definitive MRI detected a 5 mm enhancement on my right breast at eight or nine o'clock. While they would usually just have me follow up with another MRI in six months, McKeen says they don't play around with *BRCA* patients. I am scheduled Tuesday for a targeted ultrasound, and from that it will be determined if biopsy is needed. Oy again!

Psychologist: The protocol is that I need to see a psychologist, as there are ramifications to undergoing these prophylactic surgeries. My children need to consider certified genetic counseling and genetic testing at age twenty-five. For *BRCA*-positive females, the new standard is to start breast monitoring then too.

Anyone need a drink?

I am sticking with chocolate and an occasional Xanax to alleviate stress.

Let's all breathe.

Love you all,
:) xxoo
Amy

• • •

Kristin's breast cancer came back.
Dr. McKeen, Kristin's doctor too, had only seen two women in twenty-five years have a breast cancer relapse after having a child.

(Dr. McKeen said there is no data or any studies showing that having a child after breast cancer diagnosis leads to recurrence of breast cancer. It's more likely the result of faulty genes.)

For Kristin, having a child was a deeply personal decision. It was worth any amount of risk.

Kristin began the PARP clinical trial at Dana Farber in Boston with Dr. Winer. The PARP inhibitors trial was the last hope—nothing else had helped. She would have to fly up there every Friday for eight weeks and have endless tests and blood work. That's two months, ten flights, and eighteen-hour days.

Kristin began the trial, and her nodes were being managed.

> I just want to be healthy again. This is truly the greatest challenge I've ever had in my life. It's just so overwhelming sometimes to deal with cancer; it's constantly with you all the time. When faced with this type of adversity, you learn how good, good can feel. The simple things become so precious. My greatest hope is to have a boring day. All I want is to live, not survive.
>
> —Kristin

Journal Entries and Emails
JANUARY–JUNE 2010

When women take care of their health they
become their own best friend.[1]
—*Maya Angelou*

JANUARY 24, 2010

My big appointment was Thursday with Dr. McKeen. Jon and I both felt as if we had been hit by a truck afterward. I managed to have the best two nights' sleep I'd had in a long time. The week prior, I had all my girlie appointments: annual with transvaginal ultrasound, mammogram with ultrasound, and this year's breast MRI. All was good—normal, so to speak. However, my ob-gyn called me on a Friday night and read me the breast MRI report. There was a 5 mm enhancement on my right breast at eight or nine o'clock. The recommendation was to repeat the MRI in six months to notate any changes. I told him, *"Enhancement* doesn't really sound good."* My ob-gyn explained that techs have their own language and that if there was something they felt needed an immediate biopsy and was not benign, they would have noted that.

Dr. McKeen felt otherwise. She and her colleagues, not ones to play around with *BRCA* patients, suggested a targeted ultrasound with possible biopsy.

I'm up late researching tonight and found three really great tools: a documentary DVD from PBS called *In the Family*—not to be confused with *All in the Family* and Archie Bunker.

I found the www.bebrightpink.com website and the Facing Our Risk of Cancer Empowered website (www.facingourrisk.org). I signed up on the Bright Pink website to be matched with a peer sponsor who will be my sort of pen pal or buddy through this process.

JANUARY 25, 2010

This Monday I feel a bit anxious. My targeted mammogram ultrasound is tomorrow. Based on that, they will decide if I need a biopsy. And based on any biopsy result, it will be determined if it's nothing or if there is cancer there. Also, that will basically decide my surgery plan (meaning if cancer is found); I will do my breasts first and hysterectomy second. I already just really want them off. At forty, I finally *love* my breasts and am fine with my body, only now to undergo a complete change. Oh well, they are just boobs!

JANUARY 26, 2010

Today is my targeted breast ultrasound. Jon's mom, Marla (aka Grammy), is going with me at the urging of Sista. Sista thought it was in my best interests to bring moral support and someone who loved me to my appointment. I had planned on going alone. They are zooming in on the 5 mm "enhancement" that they found in the MRI. It will be determined whether they biopsy or not.

Now I'm going to color my hair and take a hot shower. Patti, the therapist, or the shrinky-dink as I like to call her, called today to schedule my psych evaluation/appointment. I will meet with her February 9. It's a requirement I meet with a therapist before the preventive oophorectomy and hysterectomy surgery.

JANUARY 27, 2010

I woke up yesterday to what may be one of the very last menstrual cycles I'll ever have—and I am sad. Why am I sad about a thing that has been known to me and many others as "the curse," "the rag"? It is the thing that makes my husband jet out of the room because he knows the verbal beating he's in for when he realizes, *Uh-oh, it's her time of the month—I'd better stay away!* This monthly occurrence has only given me awful headaches, cramps, bloating, irritability, and terrible inconvenience over the years. So ultimately I should be thrilled to be done with it. However, I am viewing it as a death, a real mortality check that my youth is slowly going behind me and the next chapter of my life is starting.

The targeted breast ultrasound appointment was nothing less than irritating. First, on the prescription, the right breast and MRI results were not noted. The tech starts chatting about her kids (*Shut up and focus on my ultrasound, lady!*) and asked why I was back; was there a history in my family? So, when I said I had a *BRCA* gene mutation, I was mystified that she looked so clueless about it. Even though it was a targeted ultrasound, she did my whole right breast. I was lying on my back. She said she did this because in the MRI you are on your stomach, and the spot may have moved slightly. I wondered why she didn't just have me lying on my stomach so we could get the same spot as the MRI. Doesn't that sound like it would make sense? She said she didn't see anything. She then ran it over to the radiologist, who did not come in the room this time. He didn't see anything either. So, what does that mean? The first ultrasound didn't show anything either. Then the MRI did. So was this a pointless appointment? Shouldn't I have had a targeted MRI and biopsy, period?

FEBRUARY 1, 2010

I got a call on a Saturday telling me how to proceed next with getting my scans so I can bring them to the expert radiologist. While the woman I ended up talking to is probably excellent, her phone manner left a lot to be desired. Not that she was mean. On the contrary, she was very friendly, but she giggled like a ditzy eighties valley girl. At one point she said, "Oh, sorry, someone was talking to me. I would tell her to stop, but she makes great coffee." She went on, "Oh, I'm so retarded. I'm so retarded." And she kept saying that over and over again—not very PC of her. I thought, *What if I had a special needs sister, brother, or family member?*

Dealing with this woman taught me that I really need to take charge of my own destiny, be my own advocate—so I am going to call up the office myself and make sure I can pick up my scan, ultrasound, and MRI disc soon.

Last week I ordered two DVDs of *In the Family*, one for my sister and one for me. It was a documentary on PBS about *BRCA* and cancer. I was very excited I found the film and had another piece of information besides Jessica Queller's book.

Went to a party last night and saw some friends I had not seen in a while. I asked my friend Gali how Monica was doing. Gali replied, "She died three months ago." I had known Monica had brain cancer. I brought her dinner last year. Gali then gave me some inspirational words. She also told me that her best friend Beth had been living with lung cancer for four years. It just reminded me that cancer is everywhere.

FEBRUARY 8, 2010

I had my appointment with the expert radiologist last week. The atmosphere of the waiting area in the office itself was friendly and professional: mahogany paneling, M&M's and other snacks for your enjoyment, a water fountain. My mother-in-law, Marla, once again went with me. Sista had suggested I take someone since one never knows what the medical professionals are going to say. Could be bad news. "Amy" is called, and I get up to walk a few steps and enter what looks like a secret government basement room. I am now staring at the ultimate patient movie experience; my tits on IMAX. There are screens everywhere, all with pictures of my tits.

I managed to refrain from turning to my mother-in-law and blurting out, "Well, here's what your son gets to fondle!"

The radiologist was warm, kind, and inviting, the polar opposite of the dark, slightly ominous room. I immediately wanted him to be my grandpa. He showed us the enhancement of my right breast and assured me it was clearly a lymph node with vessels. He said he wouldn't even biopsy it if someone insisted. I, of course, had to speak up and ask if he was sure because I am that woman who gets the rare thing. I happened to be the one in one hundred thousand who got a brain tumor back in 1998 and the one who, after getting the mumps vaccine at eleven years old, got the mumps. He assured me again. So with a big sigh of relief, my mother-in-law and I walked out of the office. And instead of going for a celebratory shot of whiskey or vodka, we went to grab a bite of lunch.

My defenses must have gone down after that because for the last week I've been battling a yucky, phlegm-induced cold and cough. I must get better so I can jump on the airplane to attend my sister's fiftieth birthday celebration in Los Angeles. It's a monumental celebration, not only for the age and year but also for all she has been through the last year and a half.

I have to sleep now. The shrinky-dink therapy appointment is in the morning.

• • •

From: Amy Byer Shainman
Sent: February 3, 2010
To: Family

Just filling you in . . .
A big sigh of relief because I don't have to have a biopsy.
Whew.
This is a process, and hopefully a plan will come soon.

Love ya,
:) Amy

• • •

When Valerie, Norene's daughter, learned about my family and the *BRCA* gene mutation, she was inspired to see a certified genetic counselor herself. Before the *BRCA* gene mutations were discovered, Valerie, as well as her mom's sisters, opted to remove their breasts (i.e., they had prophylactic—"preventive"—mastectomies).

> There is a huge hole in my soul. I am a motherless daughter! You cannot live through what I experienced and not spend a lifetime wondering, *Am I next?* I had my mind made up long before I was thirty to have surgery to remove my breasts.
> Valerie, Norene's daughter

Seeing what our family had learned, Valerie wanted the available genetic information for herself and her two sons. Valerie met with a certified genetic counselor and tested negative for a *BRCA* gene mutation. However, other relatives have not been tested, so while Valerie is negative for a *BRCA* mutation, there still could be a *BRCA* mutation within her family, one that Valerie simply did not inherit. Valerie is also continuing to touch base with her genetic counselor yearly to ask about newly discovered genes associated with hereditary cancer.*

• • •

From: Valerie
Sent: February 4, 2010
To: Amy Byer Shainman

Hi, Amy,
I was surprised to hear from the geneticist so fast and am equally surprised that my *BRCA* test was negative. I am so happy that I finally had the test, and I thank you for your encouragement. Now I can focus all my good thoughts on you and Jan.
How are you?

XO,
Valerie

• • •

* The field of genetic counseling and testing is constantly evolving. New tests and better techniques become available, and recommendations for carriers and non-carriers alike evolve as new data are published. For this reason, it is important to stay in contact with a genetic counselor or someone familiar with the field.
—Ellen Matloff, MS, CGC, My Gene Counsel

• • •

From: Kristin Hoke Cecere
Sent: March 3, 2010
To: Friends

Hi.
I am sorry I am writing all of this in an email to all of you. (I haven't updated my email address since Bella was born!) I hope I didn't forget anyone.

So . . .

There is no way around all of this. This is serious but doable. Up until last week, I had one small tumor in my left lung and a handful of small tumors in my head. The chemo was crossing the blood-brain barrier, and the tumors were staying the same or shrinking. Then I all of a sudden starting getting weird muscle and vision changes on one side of my face—sort of palsy and twitching, like I had last fall (that went away last year). They instantly sent me to a brain MRI last Friday. The scan showed nothing had changed in the existing tumors—all the same size or smaller (but one had advanced a bit): no big deal. But the stroke-like conditions may be indicating that my body is fighting the cancer now on the meningeal level—microscopically. I did a spinal tap today to see if they can find floating cancer in my spinal fluid. I should get those results back tomorrow (Thursday). If they proceed with treatment, it will be straight to the fluid area with a port. It would be another port (like my body one) installed in a quick surgery. And once the skin heals, [it will be] almost undetectable.

I know this is all scary, but I spoke with Dr. McKeen today, and she said she is very hopeful for me doing the chemo and possible radiation targeted to that specific area because I have gotten rid of almost fifty tumors and have always reacted to chemo.

This is still very up in the air until they know more. But my oncologist (McKeen) is at a conference in Miami right now and told me today she will see the head of oncology in Boston (my old doctor who knows me firsthand) and talk with him about it all in person. He is a great expert—he is the head US scientific adviser for the Komen Foundation. If the chemo works, I will know within a few weeks (they can test my fluid through the port). So that is good, because all the brain MRI shows right now is that there is a darkening of the tissues—a thickening—in that lower head area. So they will know more in the next two days.

Here's the tough part. If the chemo doesn't work, I have a 10 percent chance of making it. I would have six to twelve months left. Whew, that is hard to even wrap my brain around.

But the most important thing to remember [is that] my mom was given a 10 percent chance and made it seventeen years. I refuse to go down without a fight.

Look at what I have done so far. It is nothing short of a miracle that I am still here.

I know this is shocking and terrifying, but this is not it. I refuse that.

Please give me a few days to get my bearings.
If you want to email me, what I need right now is [to hear] how you all are doing with your families. Positive thoughts count. I want to hear!
(Also, keep your eye out for a Facebook page with private settings!)
As I tell Bella every night, Mommy loves you always and forever.

● ● ●

From: Kristin Hoke Cecere
Sent: March 8, 2010
To: Friends

Wow, has it been a week. Last Tuesday, I was ready to pack it up. Then I remembered I have a Disney trip coming up in a week!

I just finally inked what my plans were in the last hour.

So, because there is no conclusive evidence, I am moving forward with spinal fluid chemo. The floating cancer is too microscopic, and my spinal fluid keeps coming back clear for what they have sampled. (They could have drawn a clear area on the spine and missed it.) There is no pretest known to humankind that can see the microscopic stuff. I still have acute nerve symptoms that concern [my doctors].

So, Wednesday night Eric and I are flying to Boston to have another neuro-oncologist meet with me Thursday at 8:00 a.m. at Dana Farber. I am already scheduling surgery Friday at their sister hospital across the street, Brigham Women's Hospital, because I think I will need it. They are going to do a very basic surgery—one hour—and it will put in a port in my head. After my skin heals in that tiny patch, I will have about a millimeter raised in the hair that grows over. I will have my first "intrathecal" chemo treatment straight to that port in Boston to make sure they are getting good return and flow. Then from there on out, Florida doctors can draw on that spinal fluid port to see if there are any floating cancer cells—a much better test that is conclusive.

I plan to react to this chemotherapy, based on everything so far. So this is just a way for me to get going and do this.

I will come to work tomorrow and sign any disability papers. It would be good to just do that and get it done—one less thing! I drop Bella off at school at eight thirty and can stop by anytime. Just text me a time and [let me know] if tomorrow works for you.

I have never not kicked butt on this and don't plan to start anytime soon. The 10 percent survival rate is only if I don't react to chemo.

Don't is not in my vocabulary.
I love you all.

Kristin

• • •

From: Amy Byer Shainman
Sent: March 12, 2010
To: Kristin Hoke Cecere

Kristin,
Jon and I want to send love and strength your way!
I have to tell you, you are truly inspiring to me.
I just scheduled my surgery (hysterectomy and BSO—bilateral salpingo-oophorectomy) for March 24, and your courage gives me strength for that surgery and all that lies ahead for me too.
I will expect us to have a pretend food lunch in Brooke, Ben, and Bella's upstairs restaurant again soon!

Love, love, love,
Amy

• • •

From: Amy Byer Shainman
Sent: March 12, 2010
To: Family

Hello, My Family,

Just letting you know I am scheduled for a hysterectomy and BSO (bilateral salpingo-oophorectomy) March 24. Sista is coming the seventeenth—and I am sooooo thankful! Not really looking forward to the surgery or hot flashes, but this needs to be done! Much love.

xxxooo,
Amy

• • •

From: Valerie
Sent: March 14, 2010
To: Amy Byer Shainman

Hi, Amy,
Oh, who needs those parts anyway?
How are they doing the surgery?
It is so great that Jan is going to be with you!
I will be thinking of you and will be anxious to hear how you are as soon as you are up to it.
Keep your chin up and know that you have lots and lots of people thinking about you!

Lots of love!
Valerie

• • •

From: Kristin Hoke Cecere
Sent: March 23, 2010
To: Amy Byer Shainman

I am so glad you decided to schedule—good for you (this Wednesday!).
When I come up for air, I am doing the same thing!
I will not bug you during your all-important rehab, but soon after Easter week I expect to have an imaginary and real lunch at your place!

Love you two,
Kristin

• • •

APRIL 6, 2010

While I was in the pre-op area awaiting surgery, the gravity of what I was about to do hit me hard. I was not going to be able to have any more children. A wave of sadness overcame me. I saw our friend Tiffany in the corridor, and she waved to Jon and me; she was at the hospital visiting her mom.

I didn't have to do this surgery now. Surgery was a choice. I didn't have to choose to do this right now. The thought of jumping up out of bed and running out of the hospital crossed my mind more than once. I could wait. I could definitely wait, and I could have another child. If I got pregnant soon, I would have the baby at forty-one or forty-two, and after that, I could have my ovaries and uterus out. It really isn't too long of a time to wait. I could do it. I could just get up and get out of the pre-op bed, and Jon could take me home.

But something was holding me down, both a physical and an emotional weight, an arm on my thigh not letting me get up and a voice saying, *You need to do this. It's time to do this; it's not smart for you to wait.* I heard Lillian loud and clear, saying, *This is what you need to do to be here, Amy. You need to do this to be here. Do what I couldn't do: Go save your life.*

The surgery itself went well, I was sedated in pre-op and well under general for the whole thing. So, I don't really remember much, except for the first hour or so of pre-op, being in the recovery room, and then my two-night kid-free "vacation stay" in the hospital. The one thing the therapist advised me on the surgery, which is the best piece of advice and has stuck with me, is "Make sure you are at peace with your decision—whatever that is. Once they roll you into surgery, once it is done, it is done. There is no going back. You have to make sure you are at peace with whatever you decide."

It's been two weeks since my total hysterectomy and BSO. The surgery part is over but the night sweats and insomnia have begun. I had to call my doctor's office to ask them to prescribe me a sleeping pill for a few weeks until my next appointments. Perhaps then I will go on some sort of hormone or figure something out. My sister is encouraging bioidentical à la Suzanne Somers. I really haven't researched this much. For some reason on this whole *BRCA* issue, information, and surgeries, I can't seem to do my usual multitasking. I'm taking a "one day at a time" approach. In any case, I will do whatever I need to do to feel better and whatever is safest for me to do. I will figure it out.

APRIL 19, 2010

I am looking over sessions for the FORCE network conference in Orlando this June.

I feel amazing. My only side effects from surgical menopause are that my feet get *hot* at night—so much so that I have to get up and run them under cold water from the bathtub! I googled this and found that this is a real thing; it's something called *hot foot syndrome*! I am not crazy. It is a syndrome that actually exists! Also, I can't sleep (I have insomnia) unless I take a sleeping pill. There have been a few mornings where I wake up with my shirt wet—but just a few. I am beginning to think hormones, in general, are overrated! My skin is luminous and porcelain-doll clear. That alone makes me happy!

I will get my EEG and brain MRI this week—an entirely different medical reason and surgery. I scheduled an appointment because getting that out of the way will allow me to focus on "da breasts" and not worry about my brain scans for another two to three years.

If you are a parent, most likely at one time or another you have said, "I would do anything for my child. I would jump in front of a bus." By having the hysterectomy and BSO, I know I have jumped in front of the bus and made the ultimate sacrifice as a mother—for my kids. I did want a third child. But I feel I have a parental responsibility to be here for the kids I already have. When I look at it this way, I feel pretty good and rather proud of myself for doing what I did. My doctors told me, "You did the right thing. Ovarian cancer is the ultimate killer. You do not mess with it at all."

I feel strongly that dying cannot be my path. I just have to be here for myself, my kids, and my husband. With my lifetime risk for ovarian cancer as high as 50 percent, I just couldn't gamble with the silent thunder of that disease, especially since there are still no accurate surveillance methods to detect it. I knew deep inside that my sister got lucky. I couldn't play Russian roulette with my life. I had to do what was in my best interests—remain breathing.

I plan to have a prophylactic bilateral mastectomy with reconstruction next. So I will be jumping in front of the bus and be my own best friend again soon.

• • •

From: Amy Byer Shainman
Sent: May 12, 2010
To: Girlfriends

Gals,
Please come have coffee (yum!), breakfast, and a mommy moment.
See attached.
Let me know if you can make it!

xxoo,
Amy

• • •

From: Kristin Hoke Cecere
Sent: May 14, 2010
To: Amy Byer Shainman

Sorry I couldn't come. My sister was in town from Michigan.
Hope all went well!
Kristin

• • •

JUNE 7, 2010

Kristin is in hospice, dying. Her impending death hits me in a deep place. It makes me want to go cut my tits off right now.

JUNE 9, 2010

Kristin is gone.

> We thought the cancer was over. I think the cancer came back when Kristin was pregnant with Bella. She had bad chest pains. After Bella was born, [Kristin] had a scan, and the cancer had eaten away almost all her bone. There was a node in her lung. It came back in her sternum. So Kristin went back on chemo. The nodes were removed from the lung—radiation. She was back on chemo and then in remission for a second time.
>
> The PARP inhibitor Dana Farber clinical trial with Dr. Winer was Kristin's last hope—nothing else had helped. Although it looked like it helped initially and that her nodes were being "managed," on one Friday when she went up and got a scan, the cancer had grown like fire. It was bad. I think that was the beginning of the end. At that point, I felt I was watching her die, but in the back of my mind, I never thought she would. Dr. Winer said, "This is serious when nodes go to the brain," and the cancer was outside the brain.
>
> Kristin's doctor called when we were at Legal Seafoods in downtown Boston. That's when I kind of knew it was over. *So this is it; she's gonna die.* Dr. McKeen told her she had three months to live.
>
> —Eric Cecere, widower of
> Kristin Hoke Cecere

PART IV
PERENNIAL PATIENT

CHAPTER
—— 10 ——

Dr. Rimmer

History, despite its wrenching pain, cannot be
unlived, but if faced with courage,
need not be lived again[1]
—Maya Angelou

I remember the day Kristin's oncologist told her there was nothing more they could do. Kristin looked at me with tears in her eyes and said, "I'm dying." I stood there in disbelief, shook my head, and said, "No, that can't be. There's got to be some treatment you haven't tried." Her laugh was infectious. She was quite the jokester, and she was just fun to be around. That was our Kristin. She had been a part of my every day for so many years. Hers was the first face I saw at 3:30 every morning. I was lucky enough to sit beside her as her coanchor and even luckier to stand by her side on her wedding day. Not a day goes by that I don't think about her. She is missed by so many. I keep a picture of us from her wedding day on my desk. I look at it often and smile. Kristin looked so beautiful that day and was so happy and full of love. And that is how I choose to remember her.

—Felicia Rodriguez, news anchor,
friend of Kristin

Kristin was diagnosed in 2004. In the five and a half years she had breast cancer, she underwent almost twenty procedures, including two brain surgeries, one lung biopsy, radiation, several gamma knife treatments, and vocal cord injections. She spent two of those five and a half years on chemotherapy.

Her funeral was more like all her friends just hanging out in the room of the funeral home, sharing stories, comforting one another. There were flowers and a couple of posters with pictures; more flowers were on top of a casket, although she was cremated. A private family service was to be held the next day. At the funeral home, all of us chatted, hugged, and looked ridiculously sad.

I struggled that afternoon to find something to wear to the funeral home, because it had only been three months since my surgery. Everything I put on made me look huge or pregnant. I figured a black floral-like dress would be simple, and the print would mask my postsurgery waistline.

I was wrong.

Jon and I entered the funeral home and immediately saw one of his former colleagues. Upon seeing me, her eyes and hands immediately drifted down to my belly. Thinking I was pregnant, she excitedly smiled from ear to ear and let out a congratulatory "Ohhhhhhhh!"

Playfully mimicking her tone and chuckling with slight embarrassment, I immediately cut her off with my voice and my hands. "Noooooooo, it's just hysterectomy belly. I'm recovering from surgery." She looked completely mortified.

"No worries," I said.

As Jon and I gave more hugs and went on to chat with the rest of the group, Kristin's sister Patty and I locked eyes. "Amy!" she called out, and with that, we embraced in a big, tight, Kristin-type hug. "I was just talking about you! Dr. Rimmer, this is Amy. Amy, this is Dr. Rimmer."

> It is really hard (still) to put into words all of my feelings about the years that Kristin fought cancer. I think the most important thing to remember about my sister was not the cancer but her—her strength, undying spirit, tenacity, grace, optimism, and hope, and all the love she had for her family. I still miss my sister. Bella needs to remember that she was in her mother's thoughts every day and in everything Kristin did. Kristin loved her more than life itself. Bella was Kristin's gift from God.
>
> Patty Hoke Simpson, Kristin's sister

For the next hour, breast surgeon Dr. John Rimmer talked with me softly and genuinely. He educated me about BRCA and breast cancer risk right in the midst of Kristin's funeral. Honestly, I don't remember the details of our hour-long conversation except for one particular thing that cemented itself into my brain. Dr. Rimmer pointed to Kristin's picture and flowers on top of the casket and uttered words that would haunt me and save me all in the same breath: "Don't let this be you."

Kristin Hoke was diagnosed with an early stage left breast cancer and treated with breast conservation including lumpectomy and sentinel lymph node biopsy. The breast cancer was a triple-negative and poorly differentiated. Triple-negative is a more aggressive type of breast cancer, which tends to go faster and spread earlier. Triple-negative means that the cancer cells are negative for the estrogen receptor, the progesterone receptor, and the HER-2/neu receptor. Normal breast cells have estrogen and progesterone receptors on them, which makes them able to be stimulated by a woman's normal hormones, and this explains the development of the breast during puberty when these hormones are increasing.

The HER-2/neu receptor is the human epidermal growth factor receptor and at low levels is normal. When these receptors are absent or "triple-negative," the cancer cells are more abnormal and therefore more aggressive. This is understood by considering that breast cancer cells are derived from a woman's normal cells, which develop mutations and express abnormal behaviors. The normal breast cells lose many normal characteristics and develop abnormal characteristics, for example, being able to spread through tissues and not going through the normal cell cycle of division and cell death. Triple-negative breast cancers are more common in *BRCA1* and *BRCA2* mutation carriers than in nonmutation carriers.

Unfortunately, Kristin did not survive despite aggressive multimodality treatment for breast cancer, which included surgery, chemotherapy, and whole breast radiation. Despite these effective treatments, and most likely related to the aggressive type of breast cancer, her cancer recurred.

—John A. P. Rimmer, FACS, FRCS, breast surgeon

I spent the summer of 2010 with my handy white notebook orchestrating consultations with a total of six doctors; three different breast surgeons and three different plastic surgeons. I was going to need a breast surgeon to perform my mastectomy and a plastic surgeon to complete my breast reconstruction. I had learned the value of getting a second and even third opinion from previous medical issues. My Bon Jovi music-loving friend who also happens to be named Amy accompanied me to my appointments and acted as my secretary.

MY FIRST BREAST SURGEON CONSULTATION

First, I went to see Dr. Rimmer. I must have gone back to him ten times. Well, it was only three times, but it felt like ten times. Each time I went back, he was welcoming. He was still happy to see me and always prepared to answer my questions. He would draw me an adorable little grid showing where my incisions would be and then tell me exactly how and where he would remove my breast tissue. Dr. Rimmer's kind demeanor and English accent were both calming and charming; his reputation and résumé, stellar and impressive. He was a skilled surgeon who made it clear he gave a shit about me.

Prophylactic mastectomy remains the most effective way of preventing breast cancer in *BRCA1* and *BRCA2* mutation carriers. The options faced by a woman with a deleterious *BRCA1* or *BRCA2* mutation are as follows:

The first option is increased surveillance, which includes mammogram, ultrasound, and MRI, alternating every six months. It's important to note that this does not actually prevent breast cancer. The plan is to identify cancer as early as possible in order to have a good prognosis. Unfortunately, some breast cancers, including triple-negative and HER-2-positive cancer, often have a poor prognosis even when diagnosed at an early stage.

The second option is chemoprevention with tamoxifen, which is used in women with increased risk of breast cancer, including atypical hyperplasia. The documented research proving an effective reduction of breast cancer in *BRCA1* patients with this modality is somewhat lacking.

The third option is risk reduction mastectomy or prophylactic mastectomy. The aim of this surgical procedure is to remove all of the breast tissue. Research shows that prophylactic mastectomy is associated with a very significant decrease in the chance of a breast cancer occurring. Research also shows the chance of a breast cancer occurring following this procedure is in the very low single digits.

—Dr. John A. P. Rimmer

"In a nipple-sparing, skin-sparing mastectomy," Dr. Rimmer began, his hands hovering over my bare breasts to illustrate, "what I will do is go in—the incision is a half-moon starting at the top of your nipple—and then extend that incision about four inches from your nipple to your underarm."

So I could wrap my head around it, he explained it one more time.

"Dr. Rimmer, why can't the incision be under my breast like this?" I asked, showing him photos of a woman who had undergone a preventive (also called preventative or prophylactic) mastectomy. Her incision was under her breasts, and her boobs looked beyond spectacular, absolutely the perfect outcome in my mind.

I still had more opinions and more questions, as follows:

- "I want my boobs to look like this!"
- "Why doesn't she have scars?"
- "Why doesn't she have the half-moon incision?"
- "What is the reasoning behind the incision you want to do, as compared to where her incisions are—under the breast?"

Dr. Rimmer patiently answered all of my questions, going back and forth between looking me directly in the eye and further illustrating his points by showing me on my own body. "Your breast tissue can go from your chest to underneath your arm. It can go up and around, from the side here, to reach up in the chest area, which is a lot closer than having to reach from underneath your breast all the way up to your chest area." Dr. Rimmer continued, "As a breast surgeon, my goal is to get the most tissue out. The incision here is the best way to achieve that."

> Much of the discussion with women who have not had breast cancer surrounds cosmetics.

> Patients want to look good—"normal." They
> want to have a really good outcome.
> —Dr. John A. P. Rimmer

I was comforted knowing Dr. Rimmer was going to be aggressive in getting my breast tissue out—and that *that* was his primary concern. However, I still had more questions.

So I asked, "Why do you only cut halfway around the nipple? Why don't you take the nipple off and reattach it?"

> We are always going to see sporadic breast
> cancers. The genetic breast cancers I see are
> typically aggressive breast cancers with a bad
> prognosis, triple-negative breast cancers. Of
> course, any breast cancer can come back/
> recur. Preventing breast cancer from starting
> so it can't come back and it can't kill you [is
> a better option]. The best breast cancer is
> the breast cancer that you don't get. One is
> better off not even having it. For the genetic
> group, there is the option of prophylactic
> mastectomy.
> —Dr. John A. P. Rimmer

Again Dr. Rimmer calmly explained, "Well, you have to maintain the blood supply to the nipple. There is always a risk in this type of surgery that you will lose the nipple, that the nipple will not survive; we call that nipple death or necrosis. There is always that risk with this surgery. There are certain criteria that the plastic surgeon and I go through to deem if you are going to be a good candidate for the nipple-sparing, skin-sparing mastectomy with reconstruction."

The effectiveness of the prophylactic mastectomy depends on the thoroughness of the resection of the breast tissue. We are unable to predict a 100 percent risk reduction. Surgery is always a balance between risks and benefits, and a too aggressive surgical approach increases the risk of complications. For example, in a *BRCA1*-positive patient, bilateral salpingo-oophorectomy [BSO] reduces the risk of breast cancer by approximately 50 percent if done prior to natural menopause. Having this surgery before natural menopause would bring a *BRCA1* patient's breast cancer risk down from approximately 85 percent to 42 percent. Having prophylactic mastectomy further reduces cancer risk to very low single digits (about 3 percent). A *BRCA*-positive patient's cancer risk then becomes significantly less than the average woman's risk for developing breast cancer in her lifetime (average risk is considered about 12 percent lifetime risk, or one in eight women). If a *BRCA*-positive woman were to present with breast cancer, she might elect to have a nipple- and areola-sparing mastectomy. Also, she may need chemotherapy, radiation therapy, and hormonal therapy. All of these treatments are designed to reduce the risk of breast cancer recurrence, but they all have significant side effects. Despite all of these aggressive treatments, the breast cancer can recur and affect the survival of the patient. If we compare this to a *BRCA*-positive woman who does not yet

have cancer and is having a prophylactic mastectomy, there would be no other aggressive
treatments, and in effect this high-risk individual would be treated only with surgery. The
effectiveness of risk reduction or prophylactic
mastectomy is considered to be the same in
BRCA1 and *BRCA2* patients.

—Dr. John A. P. Rimmer

The whole time Dr. Rimmer was thoroughly and gently explaining everything, my fabulous friend Bon Jovi Amy was meticulously taking notes. Completely overwhelmed with all the information, I was beyond thankful that Bon Jovi Amy was there with
me and willing to write things down.

Some of the best advice I ever received was to make sure I had
someone at appointments with me taking notes. There is so much
information to absorb, and it can be quite paralyzing. While you are
listening to what seems like never-ending information and details,
most of the time you feel you are in a fog. You can't believe that
you are at an appointment discussing having a mastectomy when
you don't have cancer.

Well, you don't have cancer yet . . .

That is the whole reason I want to do this, isn't it? Because if I can
help it, I don't ever want to get breast cancer! If I do this surgery,
my breast cancer risk would drastically reduce and would be less
than that of the general population. The general female population
has a breast cancer risk of about 12 percent. I would be going from
as high as 85 percent lifetime risk of getting breast cancer down
to about 3 percent breast cancer risk. While my head was telling
me this surgery was the smart thing for me to do, the best chance
I had at remaining breathing, I still couldn't quite wrap my head
around it all.

MY FIRST PLASTIC SURGEON CONSULTATION

I went on to consult with Dr. Lickstein, the plastic surgeon who works with Dr. Rimmer.

> When I see a high-risk patient like Amy in my office for a breast reconstruction consultation, I am always aware of how difficult it is for women to consider choosing to remove a part of their body so closely associated with their sense of self and body image, especially when they don't have a cancer diagnosis. Through this anxiety and sense of urgency, my duty as a surgeon is to provide as much information as possible. I have found the best approach is first to educate and inform, and ensure that prospective patients are made aware of all of the types of breast reconstruction.
> Only then, after careful examination and discussion, can I design the surgical plan most likely to be successful, taking into account the patient's goals, lifestyle, and family responsibilities. I always tell patients that the more time spent before surgery, the fewer surprises they should experience once they start down the reconstructive path. These situations are one of the most challenging, and one of the most fulfilling, aspects of my plastic surgery practice.
> —David A. Lickstein, MD, FACS; Diplomate, American Board of Plastic Surgery

I was waiting for an epiphany.

What should I do, and who should my doctors be?

Waiting and waiting …

Should I even do this?

You would think after watching Sista in agony on the floor—witnessing the pain of ovarian cancer—I would be clear about what I needed to do. You would think after watching Kristin go through so many treatments for triple-negative breast cancer and still die, I would have a clear picture in my head of what I needed to do. You would think that knowing this and that each of them was *BRCA1*-positive too—well, you would think there would be a clear picture in my head of what I needed to do.

I realized I did have a clear picture in my head; it was my heart that had a hard time letting my head wrap around that idea. It was still major surgery. There were risks.

My grandmother Lillian didn't have this option of prophylactic mastectomy. She didn't know about the *BRCA* gene mutation or that there was such a thing as hereditary cancer. Lillian wasn't able to make proactive decisions to save her own life. I had to make Lillian's life mean something. Her death at a young age from breast cancer had given me information about how dangerous a *BRCA1* gene mutation can be. She'd handed me an education, an opportunity to save my life, on a silver platter. *How can I not take this opportunity?*

I had learned the science behind *BRCA* through my research and my doctors. I knew that having a *BRCA* gene mutation meant I had a high risk of getting certain cancers.

I knew I didn't want to get a cancer diagnosis that I had the power to prevent. I knew I didn't want to risk getting a triple-negative breast cancer (TNBC) diagnosis. Even if diagnosed with TNBC at an early stage, TNBC is aggressive, extremely difficult to treat, and more likely to recur after treatment. I learned that female *BRCA1* carriers who do get breast cancer, tend to get triple-negative breast cancer. I knew the facts, and I knew the faces, and they swirled around like a whirlpool in my head.

When would I feel my heart was ready to do this? How would I know who the right doctors were for me? Was my heart *ever* going to wrap around what my head was telling me to do?

A woman who is diagnosed with a *BRCA* mutation has many concerns regarding her options. It is in a patient's best interests to seek consultation with physicians experienced in the management of high-risk patients. If a patient is considering a cancer risk reduction mastectomy, it is important to find a breast surgeon with extensive experience in multiple surgical options, including nipple- and areola-sparing mastectomy with immediate breast reconstruction. It's vital to have consultations with breast surgeons and plastic surgeons who perform these procedures on a frequent and regular basis. Surgical complications in this operation are reduced when done by a surgeon who is familiar with the type of procedure and performs it on a regular basis.

The concerns regarding surgical complications are particularly in the area of infection and vascular complications. The vascular complications are reduced with a clear understanding of the vascular anatomy of the breast and with surgical techniques to minimize damage to the cutaneous blood supply.

Removing the breasts removes nerves, so patients must be informed that the sensation in the breast and nipple is not going to be what it was like before mastectomy.

> *BRCA1* and *BRCA2* mutations are the classic
> indications for risk-reduction prophylactic mas-
> tectomy, but as research finds other genetic
> mutations associated with an increased risk of
> breast cancer, prophylactic mastectomy is also
> significantly beneficial in these cases.
> It is always important for patients to obtain a
> second opinion, especially when considering
> prophylactic mastectomy.
> —Dr. John A. P. Rimmer

MY SECOND BREAST SURGEON CONSULTATION

She was hip, sharply dressed. You could tell by the breast surgeon's demeanor that she was smart as a whip, and her confident
strut in her stilettos showed she knew her way around both a designer shoe department and an operating room. Oh, how Sista
would love and approve of her killer shoes! Breast surgeon number
two was thorough, very matter-of-fact, kind, warm. There was no
reason not to like her. So I went on to meet with the plastic surgeon
with whom she worked. Bon Jovi Amy was there at these appointments with her binder, again meticulously writing notes.

> I believe that a collaborative team approach
> is critical and something a patient should ask
> about and seek out. Open communication
> between the breast surgeon, oncologist, and
> reconstructive plastic surgeon ensures that ev-
> eryone is on the same page right from the start.
> Currently, the only way to *drastically* reduce
> breast cancer risk in a *BRCA* gene carrier or
> high-risk patient is for the patient to make the
> elective choice to remove his or her breasts

before breast cancer makes the choice. The decision to take the leap and undergo a bilateral mastectomy is not an easy one, but it is made easier knowing that plastic surgeons can now achieve exceptional aesthetic results. Patients can look as natural as their preoperative state or even mimic breast augmentation.

It's in a patient's best interests to seek out a plastic surgeon with a good reputation and a great deal of experience with similar cases. It's important for a patient to feel comfortable with his or her plastic surgeon and have a sense of security knowing that everyone is in it together, even if complications or the need for revision arises.

—David A. Lickstein, MD

MY SECOND PLASTIC SURGEON CONSULTATION

This consult required that one meet with the surgeon's female assistant before meeting with him. Bon Jovi Amy and I walked into a lovely side room with a comfy couch. The female assistant was very well put together, friendly, and very pretty. However, as she began speaking, it was clear she was also as slick as an oil can. Both Bon Jovi Amy and I felt as if we were listening to a used-car salesperson. I didn't have a good vibe right then but didn't listen to my intuition and continued to meet with the surgeon in the adjacent room.

Plastic surgeon number two was friendly and thorough and explained to me his technique. Bon Jovi Amy wrote her detailed notes, and I waited. I waited for my epiphany. Was this the office where I was supposed to be? Was this my doctor? Were these my people? Why so much uncertainty?

I don't know if they're my people. I just don't know! I don't think they are my people. Okay, maybe they are my people. Shit!

> Amy was considering a prophylactic nipple-
> and skin-sparing mastectomy. What this means
> is that her breast tissue would be removed,
> virtually eliminating her risk of breast cancer.
> The entire skin envelope would remain. It is crit-
> ical that mastectomy be done by a technically
> skilled breast surgeon to minimize the risk of
> skin flap necrosis (injury). This sets the stage for
> the best aesthetic reconstructive result. With
> the healthy skin envelope preserved, if the
> breast is not too large or sagged excessively,
> an implant can be placed at the time of the
> mastectomy. The analogy is to restuffing a pil-
> lowcase. The decision to proceed with breast
> reconstruction is an individual one. Not every
> patient seen for consultation may decide to
> continue with this option. Some patients may
> find the breast reconstruction process to be
> overwhelming and choose to delay reconstruc-
> tion or not to have breast reconstruction at all.
> Each patient must choose the path that is right
> for him or her.
> —David A. Lickstein, MD

MY THIRD CONSULTATIONS

Bon Jovi Amy couldn't go with me to these third appointments. I was bummed that I was solo, but I knew the clock was ticking. *I felt the shadow of cancer hovering over me.*

In the direct-to-implant technique, we use either saline or silicone implants, and size is determined by the preoperative breast size and the patient's goals. There are round implants and an increasing array of anatomic (teardrop) shaped implants. These options give a surgeon the chance to control the final appearance of the breasts. In some cases, a patient can have an appearance very similar to that of before the mastectomy, and in others, an appearance closer to a larger-size or augmented breast. I perform a great deal of immediate reconstruction using the direct-to-implant technique and believe that this option is attractive to patients because it adds little to the hospitalization or recovery from the mastectomy. Patients can open their eyes after surgery, and the reconstruction is complete.

During this one-step direct-to-implant operation, the pectoralis muscle is elevated up off of the chest wall. The implant is placed beneath the muscle in the "subpectoral" position. A hammock, or sling, is created to support the implant using a variety of materials. Most commonly, a piece of acellular dermal matrix is placed. This is a layer of skin that has been harvested from an animal or cadaver source. *Acellular* indicates that all of the cells have been removed, eliminating the risk of transmission of any virus or diseases from the donor. The matrix provides a lattice that slowly incorporates into the tissue of the mastectomy skin flap. Over time, there is complete ingrowth and integration. While a patient is healing, the sling supports the implant, and the skin is not stressed by being under the tension of the weight of the device.

—David A. Lickstein, MD

MY THIRD PLASTIC SURGEON CONSULTATION

I liked plastic surgeon number three a lot. He was friendly and warm. Plus I got the sense that he did care about me.

The office staff led me to an elegant private changing room, where I was asked to put on an even more beautiful robe. *Is this a doctor's office or a shop on Rodeo Drive in Beverly Hills? If the fabulous office decor is any indication of how my boobs are going to look, sign me up now! Seriously, what a gorgeous facility.*

Okay, so I like this plastic surgeon! I can see this.

So, I met with the breast surgeon with whom he worked.

MY THIRD BREAST SURGEON CONSULTATION

Again, I filled out all the waiting room paperwork. *One more time, here we go: name, date, address, DOB, insurance.* Q: "Why are you here?" A: "Mastectomy, reconstruction." Medications. Medical history. *Um, no, no, no, yes, yes. Yes, no, no, no. Two C-sections, brain surgery, BRCA1 positive, family history of cancer—sister, ovarian cancer, uterine cancer; grandmother died at thirty-three.* It spewed out as a habit now; I felt like a professional patient.

By this last consult appointment, I had gone into what I can de-scribe as complete freak-out and panic mode. I was running against the clock. I was forty-one years old and was feeling I had to get this mastectomy done. I was beyond anxious and felt a tremendous sense of urgency in my head that I needed to do this. I had managed to escape having a cancer diagnosis up to this point; I just had the feeling that I had to get cancer before cancer got me. I had to have a prophylactic bilateral mastectomy before there was any chance of breast cancer, especially a triple-negative breast cancer coming into my system and possibly never getting out. How foolish I would feel and how mad at myself I would be if I didn't do this and got breast cancer. What if it was aggressive breast cancer? *Lillian and Kristin. They did not have the opportunity. I have to do this. I need to do this!*

In some instances, the breast reconstruction needs to get staged, and a tissue expander needs to be put in place. The expander is a device that is shaped similar to a breast implant and can be filled with saline over time to allow stretching of the skin. An expander is most helpful for patients with small breasts who want them to be much larger, or when a portion of the breast skin needs to be removed to excise the area of cancer. The expansion can be completed gradually, and a second operation is then required to place an implant. This is typically an outpatient procedure with a brief recovery period (one to two weeks).

Occasionally, it is important to preserve the shape of the breast while further treatment is being contemplated or completed that might affect the reconstruction, and for this we place a tissue expander. Women with large breasts that have sagged can be very challenging and have a higher risk of complications. In these cases, if a skin- and nipple-sparing mastectomy is performed, there will be excess skin that hangs too low on the chest wall. There may not be an implant of sufficient size to fill the area. A breast lift or reduction skin pattern can be used for the mastectomy to reshape the breast and place it in a more uplifted position. The tissue expander is then utilized to stretch out the breast in this improved, more aesthetic position and prepare the site for an operation to place an implant.

Other types of breast reconstruction involve the use of a patient's tissue. In some cases, the latissimus muscle is freed up from the back and tunneled through the axilla to cover a tissue expander, as this will help to mitigate the effect of radiation. I perform this procedure frequently. Breasts can also be reconstructed using a patient's own tissue. This is also known as autologous breast reconstruction, and the tissue may be obtained from the abdomen, hips, buttocks, or thighs. The early versions of these procedures tunneled the tissue from the donor site to the breast, keeping the blood supply intact. Newer flaps rely on the ability to transfer tissue and reestablish the blood supply. These flaps are based on perforating vessels and may allow immediate or delayed reconstruction without the need for an implant. They are more lengthy microsurgical procedures that require a team of surgeons and have other potential complications. For patients who are considering prophylactic mastectomy and are interested in this type of

breast reconstruction, it is crucial to seek out centers dedicated to this type of care.
—David A. Lickstein, MD

I have to be a pioneer and be brave. I have to show Sista she can do this too. Sista was still at high risk for breast cancer. However, at this point, Sista wanted no part of a preventive mastectomy.

I have to do this for Sista, for myself, for my kids. My kids!

Didn't I have a parental responsibility to do this? *As a parent, don't I have a responsibility to remain healthy for my kids?*

I have to do this soon.

Ticktock, ticktock.

I cannot die.

I thought of my Dad without Lillian.

I thought of Bella without Kristin.

I thought of my kids without me. *No. That can't happen! No!*

It was a race against the clock. I needed confirmation in my heart. But who was the right doctor? *Is this the right doctor? Is this one the right one?*

P-A-N-I-C!

The third breast surgeon came into the examining room. *Ooh,* I thought, *I'm going to like him.* Warm, fuzzy, smiley, and older—he was great! That meant he had a lot of experience.

He opened his mouth to greet me and say hello. I was psyched up, ready to start this third breast consult conversation, thinking this just might be my man. I was entirely focused on him and believed he was focused on me.

What is he going to say? Is he the one?

Ring . . . ring.

It was his cell phone.

Barely acknowledging me, he answered it.

Only later after I had processed all of my consultations did I realize that the doctor answering his phone in the middle of my consult was an enormous red flag. *My life is important!* What was going to happen if this guy were performing surgery on me and his cell phone rang? Would he pick it up? I could not say with confidence that he would not pick up his cell phone in the middle of my surgery.

However, in breast surgeon number three's office that day, in my full panic mode, I scheduled surgery with him. A massive wave of cancer fear came over me, convincing me that I had to do this and I had to do it now. It was going to be breast surgeon number three along with plastic surgeon number three, the one who would hopefully make my breasts look as spectacular as his building. I mean, I did love breast surgeon number three's technique, explanation, and recommendations. More than that, I had confidence that plastic surgeon number three would make my breasts look unbelievable.

Wasn't that my epiphany? I'd done it! I was moving forward! *Scheduled!*

I went home from that appointment and ate lots and lots of chocolate while sitting on my decision and my ever-expanding derriere. However, something, more than just my extra pounds, didn't feel right.

Shit! I was listening to that voice, that inner voice. Something was nudging me.

I called up Dr. Rimmer.

"Can I come back in to see you? I have some more questions."

> It's a big decision. It's life-changing. We want to be able to give the patient the right decision for herself and her family. It was not weird at all that Amy came in to see me again.
> —Dr. John A. P. Rimmer

It was the same scenario. I went back in. Dr. Rimmer warmly greeted me. His lovely English accent was very comforting. I wanted to understand why these other doctors had told me certain things and why Dr. Rimmer had a different plan in mind. Dr. Rimmer grabbed his notepad and again drew his little grid for me. Again Dr. Rimmer patiently explained to me, "In a nipple-sparing, skin-sparing mastectomy, what I will do is go in—the incision is a half-moon starting at the top of your nipple—and then I will extend that incision about four inches from your nipple to your underarm." As he had done before at my first appointment—so I could wrap my head around it—he explained it all yet again.

One more time I asked, "So, I want to know—why can't the incision be under my breast?" Again I asked all of my questions, and yet again, Dr. Rimmer went through it all.

> I have four sisters, a wife, and two daughters. I am sensitive to this situation, as we are talking about having your breasts removed when you don't have breast cancer. Being fearful is normal. Breasts are a complicated sociological phenomenon. It's not like your finger, thumb, or leg. Amy was a healthy person; why would she do this? When you don't have a problem, why would you go and have surgery? Prophylactic mastectomy is a difficult thing to do, and I'm sensitive to that, while offering a patient a great opportunity to avoid chemo, radiation, and metastatic breast cancer.
>
> —Dr. John A. P. Rimmer

I whipped out those postprophylactic mastectomy photos I had of my friend with the magnificent breasts.

"I want my boobs to look like this!"

"Why doesn't she have scars?"

"Why doesn't she have the half-moon?"

"What is the reasoning behind the incision?"

Clearly and yet again, Dr. Rimmer answered my questions. "That woman you know may very well have had very small breasts—a smaller amount of breast tissue to begin with. Breast tissue can go from your chest to underneath your arm, and it can go up and around. Going from the side here to reach up in the chest area is a lot closer than having to reach from underneath your breast all the way up to your chest area. You look like you have a good amount of tissue going to the side under your underarms. As a breast surgeon, my goal is to get the most tissue out. Going in this way is the best way to achieve that."

Dr. Rimmer was going to be very aggressive in getting my breast tissue out—and he was clear that *that* was his primary concern. It was mine too. His explanation made sense and gave me reassurance. "This is your opportunity, Amy, your opportunity as a *BRCA*-positive woman to cure yourself before getting cancer, before something happens," Dr. Rimmer stated clearly and candidly.

> Kristin is not here, Amy is here. Amy and Kristin are basically the same person. They both carry a *BRCA1* genetic mutation and have a family history of breast cancer. Kristin was an amazing person, the person who was going to beat breast cancer. She did everything, went everywhere, and that didn't happen. When Amy came to see me, I had Kristin on my mind. I did not want [what had happened to Kristin] to happen to Amy. Since Kristin first came to see me, there had been a paradigm change. There was more focus on family history, genetic testing; it was an exciting time. I didn't want what happened to Kristin to happen anymore. Cancer can't happen to Amy. I wish Kristin were here. We want to keep people here. If you have

a family history, identifying women with high
risk is the difference between Amy and Kristin
being on this earth. Prophylactic mastectomy
is a lifesaving opportunity for women in the
high-risk and *BRCA* community.

—Dr. John A. P. Rimmer

I heard Dr. Rimmer but was still entirely focused on the nipple.
"Why do you only cut halfway around the nipple? Why don't you
take the nipple off and reattach it?" I asked, hoping to understand
every little detail again.

"Well," he said, "you have to maintain the blood supply to the
nipple. There is always the risk in this type of surgery that you will
lose the nipple, that the nipple will not survive—necrosis. There
is always a risk with any surgery." Dr. Rimmer continued, "There
are certain criteria that the plastic surgeon and I go through to
deem if you are going to be a good candidate for the nipple-sparing,
skin sparing mastectomy with reconstruction."

There are potential complications of breast reconstruction. Some are more serious than others and can make the process much more challenging for both patient and plastic surgeon.
They may even affect the aesthetic outcome.
As with any surgical procedure, bleeding can
occur after surgery and require an emergent
return to the operating room. If the mastectomy skin flaps are left thin or not handled with
care by the breast surgeon, areas of the skin
or nipple may be injured. Superficial injuries
first seem like bruises that evolve to appear
worse over the first few days and then gradually
heal. Deeper injuries may be difficult to discern

at first but can progress and may require further surgery to trim away the involved areas. This may result in loss of the nipple or change in the shape of the reconstructed breast. In some cases, this may necessitate converting a single-stage implant reconstruction to a tissue expander and staged reconstruction.

Injured skin compromises the body's barrier to bacteria and can increase the risk of infection. Infections that occur for this or any other reason may necessitate removing the expander or implant and waiting for several months prior to replacement.

There are risks inherent to implant placement. Implants can rupture, although the rate of rupture for the current devices is very low. The FDA has recommended MRI surveillance of the implants at regular intervals to detect ruptures. The scar tissue, or capsule, that forms around an implant can become firm or even tighten (capsular contracture). This capsular contracture can change the appearance of the reconstructed breast and is often painful. It occurs much more frequently after radiation. If the skin flaps are thin after the mastectomy is complete, rippling of the implant may be visible. It is a less frequent occurrence with the development of cohesive gel (gummy bear) implant. Flap procedures have additional risks associated with the donor site.

—David A. Lickstein, MD

Wendy, my forever friend since I was five years old, came with me to this appointment with Dr. Rimmer. Dr. Rimmer went over everything again—and again for me, and then once again.

I saw Wendy's face, and then . . . *the feeling.*

Peace.

Comfort.

Lillian.

Epiphany.

Dr. Rimmer picked up the phone and called Jon to see if he had any questions.

Wow, I thought. *Amazing. What doctor does that?*

Epiphany confirmed.

My breast surgeon was Dr. Rimmer.

My plastic surgeon was Dr. Lickstein.

> Kristin Hoke's case illustrates the contrast between aggressive conventional multimodality breast cancer treatment versus risk-reduction prophylactic mastectomy prior to the occurrence of a breast cancer. She was an incredible woman who treated her breast cancer very aggressively using all modalities available, including the latest chemuthorapy trials. Despite this, she succumbed to her breast cancer. Her memory serves to encourage all of us to ensure this never happens again.
>
> It is unclear whether Kristin's having a bilateral mastectomy after her breast cancer diagnosis would have affected her prognosis. However, one thing is for sure. If she had been genetically tested and identified as a *BRCA1* mutation carrier before developing breast cancer and if she had a prophylactic mastectomy, it is

very likely she would still be alive today. Kristin was concerned about breastfeeding her child, and I can understand her concerns. My view as a physician is that a woman does not need breasts to conceive or provide nutrition for a baby in this day and age.

I see many young women at high risk of breast cancer, including *BRCA1* and *BRCA2* mutation carriers. One of their major life concerns is often about developing breast cancer. Other concerns are their body image and their role in the family. *BRCA* mutations have been present in women and men for hundreds of years. These genetic mutations have killed women and men throughout the generations. However, now there are medical options to save lives. Medical research has identified these genetic mutations. Doctors have the ability to intervene and prevent breast cancer occurring in these women and save their lives. This opportunity was not available to us previously but is available now. Hopefully, future research will provide less invasive risk-reducing options for women, but currently the prophylactic mastectomy is the most effective way to prevent breast cancer in these high-risk women. Women have died from this genetic mutation over and over throughout time, and it is time this stops. We have the medical ability to stop it.

BRCA-positive patients and those with other genetic mutations are at increased risk for multiple cancers. It is important for women and men to seek out certified genetic counselors and high-risk clinics so they may be thoroughly and accurately assessed as to their individual cancer risks. People must become their own health care advocates in this increasingly complex environment of hereditary cancer and cancer genetics.

—Dr. John A. P. Rimmer

If you decide to have breast reconstruction along with your mastectomy, it is crucial to note the "aesthetic" of the plastic surgeon. Plastic surgeons each have their own aesthetic. What this means is that what one plastic surgeon thinks looks fantastic, another plastic surgeon may say looks fair, and even another plastic surgeon may say looks horrible. While all plastic surgeons have their own aesthetic and agenda, each patient does too. It's critical for patients to know if their expectations of how their breasts will look coincide with and compare with the aesthetic of the plastic surgeon. Sometimes what a plastic surgeon thinks may look fantastic, a patient may feel looks awful! Also, does one doctor trump another in the operating room? This shouldn't be the case! The input should be equal! The goal of the surgery needs to be to get the most breast tissue out while achieving the best possible cosmetic breast reconstruction result that the patient can be happy with. It must be a team effort between both the breast surgeon and the plastic surgeon, and you must be your own advocate and ask questions.

I learned in my consultations with breast surgeons and plastic surgeons that it's important to ask them to show you their books of photos of mastectomy and reconstruction patients. Also, ask them if they have any patients who would be open to talking to you, ones who have had the same procedure done. I took in to Dr. Lickstein pictures from magazines of breasts I liked and breasts I didn't like. These pictures were a great tool that helped communicate to him

what was in my head. Jon asked me to take in a picture of Katy
Perry from the cover of *Rolling Stone*. I did, and Dr. Lickstein and I
had a good laugh about that. Showing your plastic surgeon photos
of breast shapes, sizes, and nipples—how you would ideally like to
look—is an excellent way to convey to him or her what you want.
You can see if you react the same way the plastic surgeon does to
the images. Pay attention to your surgeon's reaction. Ask the plastic
surgeon if he or she has any nipple tattoo pictures or photos of created nipples. We take pictures to our hairstylists, and this decision
is arguably much more important and more permanent.

Surgical techniques for mastectomy are always evolving, as are
breast reconstruction techniques. There is, too, always the option
of going flat: mastectomy without breast reconstruction.

CHAPTER

—— 11 ——

Fat, Tissue, Woman, Roar

SEPTEMBER 16

The whole is more than the sum of its parts.
Aristotle

Potentially Fatal
Fat and Tissue Removal Day

I was about to have potentially fatal fat and tissue removed from my chest—a nipple-sparing, skin-sparing bilateral prophylactic mastectomy with direct-to-implant breast reconstruction.

Exactly twelve years earlier, on September 16, 1998, I had potentially fatal fat and tissue removed from my brain, having previously been diagnosed with an acoustic neuroma, a brain tumor. This major brain tumor surgery also factored heavily into my decision-making process to move forward with my prophylactic mastectomy and reconstruction. I wanted to get ahead of any more medical maladies.

Back in 1998, Jon and I were finally in the same locale. We were twenty-nine years young and living on the East Coast in what I called our cozy little Gilligan's Island Florida love shack. All was good in romance and love, and we were thrilled to finally be together after dating long distance for way too long—almost three years. While Jon was starting his new job in television, I was adjusting to grocery shopping and life for two and getting our new place homey and organized.

I came down with a bad sore throat and most definitely was not 100 percent. I didn't feel well, and my ears felt clogged. I figured I had messed them up, along with my vocal cords, singing when I was sick.

A few weeks later, Jon and I went to Cape Canaveral and Kennedy Space Center. It was exceedingly hot, as it always is in Florida in the summertime, around ninety-three degrees with intense humidity. In line for one of the exhibits, I felt incredibly dizzy and started to sway. I instantly just attributed it to the heat, thinking that I was probably dehydrated.

Shortly after that, Jon walked in the door from work one night, concerned. "What is going on? I can hear the television blaring from all the way down the street! Why do you have the volume up so loud?" I didn't know what he was talking about.

"What do you mean?" I replied. I didn't realize I'd turned the volume up to the maximum level. As I started paying attention over the next few days, I realized I was really having trouble hearing people talk to me in my right ear, mainly when I was on the telephone.

I went to an ENT, and he put me on prednisone. After I explained all my symptoms, he thought I might have a virus. When the prednisone didn't clear up my hearing problem, he didn't know what else he could do for me and referred me to another doctor in the area.

I met with the second physician. I had some ear-blasting test in which I did not respond "normally." "Well," the doctor said, "it could be one of two things. Either you messed up your hearing with singing while you were sick, or—but there is really a very small chance it could be this—it is a brain tumor. But I really don't think it's a brain tumor. You have a one in one hundred thousand chance that it's a brain tumor."

I demanded the MRI because, along with not feeling well, *I felt deep in my gut that something was wrong.*

Monday morning, this time with Jon in tow, I was back at the ENT's office. The weekend had been a long, excruciating wait. As the ENT entered the exam room, he broached the subject. "Remember how I said you have a one in one hundred thousand chance? Well, you're that one. I'm so sorry. It's a brain tumor." After the ENT confirmed my intuition, he explained what type of tumor was stuck in my head. "It's an acoustic neuroma," he said, "a benign tumor that starts in your ear canal. As I said, it's benign. However, if it hits your brain stem, you're dead. So, you need to address it."

After my initial freak-out and hysteria, I researched acoustic neuroma. After getting four different surgical opinions, I had brain surgery on September 16, 1998, to remove the two-centimeter tumor from my head. I would need to follow up with brain scans every few years for the rest of my life to make sure there was no regrowth.

An acoustic neuroma (or vestibular schwannoma) is a tumor of the lining of the nerve that controls hearing and balance. There is currently no scientific evidence or research indicating an acoustic neuroma is *BRCA* related. The first study of its kind on acoustic neuromas to discover why some people develop acoustic neuroma while others do not is ongoing at Yale University under the direction of Dr. Elizabeth Claus. I have contributed my DNA to this study, the Yale University Acoustic Neuroma Study.

> Approximately one out of every 100,000 individuals per year develops a vestibular schwannoma. Unilateral vestibular schwannomas affect only

one ear [which is what I had]. Bilateral vestibular schwannomas affect both ears and are usually associated with a genetic disorder called neurofibromatosis type 2 (NF2). Scientists believe that both unilateral and bilateral vestibular schwannomas form following the loss of the function of a gene on chromosome 22. Scientists believe that this particular gene on chromosome 22 produces a protein that controls the growth of Schwann cells. When this gene malfunctions, Schwann cell growth is uncontrolled, resulting in a tumor. Scientists also think that this gene may help control the growth of other types of tumors. In NF2 patients, the faulty gene on chromosome 22 is inherited. For individuals with unilateral vestibular schwannoma, however, some scientists hypothesize that this gene somehow loses its ability to function properly.[1]

—The National Institute on Deafness and Other Communication Disorders

Given that I have to have repeated brain scans every few years, the last thing I wanted to do was to have to get breast MRIs, mammograms, and ultrasounds every six months, especially with what I had learned about triple-negative breast cancer in *BRCA1*-positive women. I discovered through my research that 75 percent of *BRCA1* mutation carriers who get breast cancer get triple-negative breast cancer and that 30 percent of the breast cancers in *BRCA2* carriers are triple-negative.

Triple-negative breast cancers are very aggressive and difficult to treat. (Less than 11 percent of breast cancers in the general population are triple-negative.) Triple-negative breast cancers almost always require chemotherapy because they lack specific cell surface proteins that can be targeted by medication. These fast-growing cancers can show up as large tumors in just a few months. Even with *BRCA*-positive patients following a protocol of a six-month screening routine that alternates between mammogram and MRI, triple-negative cancers can pop up in the interval between screening exams. This information about triple-negative breast cancer is one reason that women who carry a *BRCA* gene mutation choose to have a preventive mastectomy to reduce their breast cancer risk. The drug tamoxifen is ineffective at preventing this specific type of cancer.

Also, I learned as a *BRCA1* carrier that even though I underwent a hysterectomy and BSO, I was still going to be at risk for peritoneal cancer (the peritoneum being the lining of the abdomen). The risk is low, only about 1 percent, but it is still there. Through my support groups, I have known a small handful of *BRCA*-positive women who have been diagnosed with peritoneal cancer after having their ovaries and/or uterus removed preventatively.

I also had extremely dense breasts. I learned that having dense breasts alone increases your cancer risk. More than that, it is challenging, if not impossible, to detect cancers in dense breasts with a regular mammogram. Sista and I both had very dense breasts.

Breast density just might be the greatest cancer risk you've never heard of.

- 40% of women have dense breast tissue.
- Breast density is one of the strongest predictors of the failure of mammography to detect cancer.
- Mammography misses every other cancer in dense breasts.
- Breast density is a well-established predictor of breast cancer risk.

- High breast density is a greater risk factor than having two first degree relatives with breast cancer.
- The vast majority of women are unaware of the density of their breasts.
- 95% of women do not know their breast density.
- Less than one in 10 women learn about their dense breast tissue from their doctors.

Additional screening tests to mammography for women with dense breast tissue will nearly increase detection by up to 100%. These invasive cancers, missed by mammography, are small, node-negative and at an *early* stage.[2]
    —Are You Dense Advocacy, Inc.

I was informed about my high risk of getting breast cancer due to my *BRCA1* gene mutation. I also now had the knowledge that I had very dense breasts. There was no way I could live with the daily anxiety of continually wondering, *Is this the day I am going to get breast cancer?* I did not want a life of breast and brain scans. I was going to do whatever was in my power to avoid a cancer diagnosis.

My life was not my own. I had children. I needed to be here for Brooke and Ben. I felt a huge, nagging push and a parental responsibility to be here for them and have a prophylactic mastectomy. I needed to make the smart decision as a parent. *Isn't it in their best interests for me to do this? Isn't it my responsibility to make all attempts to remain alive for my children?* I felt I had to ensure I was going to be there for them and not die.

I still wanted Sista to consider having a preventive mastectomy too. She had already survived two separate primary cancers, but she was still at high risk for breast cancer. However, Sista remained nowhere close to even thinking about a preventive mastectomy. She said she had been through so much already, the pain, cancer, chemo—a lot. It was difficult, but I had to respect her decision. I wanted to do the surgery not only for myself but also, feeling it was very important to be brave, to show Sista she could do it too. If I did it first, maybe that would give her the courage. If I did it first with stellar aesthetic results, then maybe she wouldn't be so against it. Even though Sista didn't want any part of having a prophylactic mastectomy, she did say she would feel foolish if diagnosed with breast cancer now, knowing all she did about *BRCA* gene mutations.

People talk about finding the cure for cancer. I felt prophylactic breast surgery was my best answer as a *BRCA1*-positive woman for "a cure." I really didn't want Sista to get another cancer diagnosis! I was hoping Sista would decide to get this "cure" too.

Sista. Kristin. Lillian. In the stillness of my private thoughts in bed at night and throughout my day, I thought of each of them. In the stillness of my private thoughts in bed at night and throughout my day, my thoughts were always the same:

I do not ever want to be a cancer patient if I can help it. I am going to do all that I can to remain not being one. I do not want to wait to get cancer and risk getting triple-negative breast cancer. Kristin had triple-negative breast cancer. I would bank on it that my grandmother Lillian had triple-negative breast cancer. I am going to do whatever I need to do to remain breathing!

More than this, the following thoughts repeatedly raced through my head. Yet I only shared them with a few close friends, as I didn't want to upset or offend breast cancer survivors or those just diagnosed with breast cancer or any other type of cancer.

I don't ever want to fucking go through chemo! I don't want to be sick from chemo, and I sure as hell don't want ever to wear some fucking colorful scarf on my bald head. Not interested! NOT FUCKING INTERESTED! I don't want to stand proudly with others in any pink race walks or call myself a survivor if I can help it. I already had my major medical malady for this life—a brain tumor. I saw BRCA firsthand, what Sista went through, what Kristin went through. Kristin died. Lillian died. I will do what is in my power and capability not to have cancer be part of my life or the path of my life. I have a high risk of getting breast cancer, and I could die from it if I do nothing. I do not want to give breast cancer any fucking opportunity to grow in my body!

I also learned 30 percent of breast cancers become metastatic, with metastasis being the spread of cancer from where it started (primary site) to other places in the body. Breast cancer is considered metastatic, or stage IV, if it has spread beyond the breast and nearby lymph nodes to other parts of the body, such as the bones, liver, lungs, brain, or other organs. At that point, the breast cancer is treatable but not curable.

Why in the world should I wait until I get breast cancer? I was forty-one years old. I had an opportunity—an opportunity that my grandmother before me did not have. I was thankful to have the maturity to know who the hell I was and that I was not going to let fat and tissue in my breasts define me or rule my world. Neither was I was going to allow others' judgment or ignorance of my decision destroy what I felt in my core was the right medical choice for me. I knew my options, and I knew the science. I was more than confident with my decision to go with the one-step direct-to-implant surgery; I had gone back and forth between types of surgery and implant types versus using my own tissue, and ultimately I had made my personal decision to go with a silicone implant. I was in touch with myself enough to know that emotionally I would feel most comfortable not waking up flat. Why should I risk getting breast cancer, risk getting triple-negative breast cancer, or risk not being here for my kids? I had utmost confidence in my doctors. Breasts did not define me; they were just one part of me. I was not going to endure a cancer diagnosis or lose my life over goddamn fat and tissue if I could help it.

Rrrrooooaaaarrrrr!

Waking up from my one-step direct-to-implant prophylactic bilateral mastectomy and breast reconstruction surgery, I felt intense
pressure. It was as if an elephant were sitting on my chest.

The pressure lessened daily, from an elephant to a rhinoceros
to a lion, then a cheetah to a large dog to a lapdog, and finally to a
small cat.

It took me about two weeks to feel somewhat normal after
surgery and six weeks to make a full recovery. However, if I'm to
be honest, the number one thing I felt when I woke up from my
one-step mastectomy and breast reconstruction surgery was *relief.*

Sista decided she was ready to move forward with a prophylactic mastectomy. In preparation for that surgery, she had a breast
MRI in January of 2011. The MRI and subsequent biopsy detected
invasive ductal carcinoma. She had breast cancer. The date of her
operation was obviously moved up. Fortunately, her cancer had
not spread. However, she endured many additional surgeries on
account of multiple breast reconstruction issues.

> Since I tested positive for a *BRCA1* genetic mu-
> tation and had been diagnosed previously with
> two separate primary cancers, my doctors were
> carefully monitoring me for breast cancer. I al-
> ternated between a mammogram and an MRI
> every six months. About one year after I under-
> went genetic testing, an MRI discovered that I
> had breast cancer. Thankfully, the breast cancer,
> found at an early stage, was ER-positive breast
> cancer, not aggressive triple-negative breast
> cancer. I elected to have a double mastectomy
> and was fortunate that I did not require che-
> motherapy. Having the genetic counseling and
> subsequent genetic testing ultimately gave me

information about my cancer risk. This knowledge about my *BRCA1* genetic mutation led to
my having very close breast surveillance after
my initial ovarian and uterine cancer diagnosis.
—Jan Byer (Sista)

PART V
REFLECTION POND

CHAPTER

—— 12 ——

Lessons of Self-Worth

My prophylactic surgeries forced me to reassess what defined me as a woman. With my female parts removed and my female parts reconstructed, what did this mean for me? Self-worth, beauty, and empowerment. As if wearing a tinted moisturizer with SPF, I was now more luminous, more authentic, and better protected. As though treated with a soothing eye cream, the crow's feet around my eyes diminished with the knowledge that I had drastically reduced my risk for future "wrinkles" in my life.

I chose to be fierce and strong, to be fearless and conquer. I decided to be here for my husband, my kids, and most importantly myself. I let go of my dream of having more children and instead took on the side effects of menopause. I said good riddance to my "ticking time bomb" breast tissue and welcomed my new breasts with implants and minimal scars. I accepted the numbness in my chest and lack of feeling in my breasts in exchange for a newfound sense of strength in my core. I became my own advocate and ultimately a pioneer in my family.

Sista's and Kristin's *BRCA*-related cancer diagnoses happened simultaneously right in front of me. As I watched their journeys, it altered my perspective on everything. For me, I saw only two choices: do nothing or do something. I could sit around with my gene mutation, my high-risk percentages, and my dense breasts and wait to see if I would get a hereditary female cancer, or I could have prophylactic surgeries and virtually cure myself before any issue of breast or ovarian cancer were to arise.

As I watched what both Sista and Kristin were going through, I thought, *Yes, I inherited this dangerous genetic mutation too, but I have an opportunity to get ahead of it, a chance to reduce my cancer risk drastically. There are options to get ahead of this and get cancer before it gets me.* Yes, the cancer risk-reducing options of prophylactic surgeries aren't great options, but they are options, and currently they are the best options a *BRCA*-positive woman has of drastically reducing her breast cancer and ovarian cancer risk. Knowing that I could do something to prevent myself from going through what each of them had gone through and even avoid death, ultimately, I could not just sit on this knowledge and do nothing.

I chose to have my prophylactic oophorectomy and hyster-ectomy and bilateral mastectomy with reconstruction surgeries within the same calendar year—2010—just six months apart. It was important to me to do these surgeries in the same year because I wanted to just get back to being a mom and resume my everyday life; I wanted the surgical operations behind me.

My view on these prophylactic surgeries was that I was remov-ing the parts of me that were causing more harm than good. This philosophy was similar to the one I'd had with my previous major surgery to remove my brain tumor, an operation that removed a benign tumor out of my head that could have caused me great harm, even death. I knew that brain surgery would cut the nerves for hearing in my right ear, leaving me entirely deaf in that ear, but by removing the tumor, I could save my own life before the tumor grew too big, hit my brain stem, and killed me. I saved my life with brain surgery, and prophylactic surgeries were going to save my life again.

My decision to have prophylactic surgeries to reduce my cancer risk was what was right for me; however, it may not be right for everyone. As my breast surgeon, Dr. Rimmer, and my oncologist, Dr. McKeen have said, there are other options for breast cancer risk reduction, including taking tamoxifen or undergoing enhanced surveillance/screenings. However, it's crucial that women understand that while there are "tools" such as a pelvic exam, transvaginal ultrasound, and CA-125 blood test, *there is no consistently reliable screening test to detect ovarian cancer.*[1]

Burying one's head in the sand is not in the best interests of one's health. So, I hope that all women and men realize that knowing their family history and learning how they can stay healthy is the most loving thing they can do for themselves and their loved ones.

> Kristin would look at me and apologize that she was going to leave us. She was always smiling, happy, like Bella. She put up with my shit. I'm difficult. She was an incredible person. Bella was her everything. I don't think she wanted to be remembered; she wanted to live a happy life, not have cancer, raise Bella, and go fishing. I remember Kristin most now when I am with Bella and our dog Pongo. Kristin loved our dog Buddy. She would really love Pongo.
>
> —Eric Cecere, widower of
> Kristin Hoke Cecere

> Kristin underwent endless cycles of chemotherapy, cycles of radiation, three brain surgeries,

and a clinical trial. All she wanted was to feel good again. To survive. For Bella. Her determination was stronger than ever. During our final interview together, she told me that she yearned for a normal, simple life free of this ravaging disease. Kristin said, "Life is too short. It is precious. You should value every day like it's your last. And if you are not doing that, you need to get busy."

—Tiffany Kenney Wiseman,
news anchor, friend of Kristin

CHAPTER

—— 13 ——

Letters and Lillian

I went back to Dad's home office closet, searching for that paper about my grandmother that I had found years earlier. I found two letters. I was so confused. I only remembered seeing one letter.

Why was it as though I was looking at these two pieces of paper for the first time? It had been nine years since I had searched through all of this. One letter was from my grandfather to a doctor, and the other letter was the doctor's reply to him. As I started reading, I understood everything with new and profound perspective. It was a complete revelation.

Feb. 1934.

Dr. ____ ____,
Washington, D.C.

Dear Doctor:

The writer was just spoken to by ____ ____ of this city on ____ I consulted an operation for cancer, and he suggested that I consulted with you regarding my wife who has been seriously ill for the last few weeks. The following information will give you an outline of the trouble.

In August 1932, she had her left breast removed entirely due to a cancerous condition, at that time there was also an appearance of a lump at the top of her shoulder which was also removed; however even after this second operation she complained at various times that it pained her where this lump was removed.

About two weeks ago she was taken ill with a severe vomiting spell and pains in her head, and complained about her eyes troubling her. She was treated for about four weeks by a medical man for neuralgia, suffering at this time with severe head pains. We then called in Dr. ____ ____ the surgeon who performed the operation, who in turn had Dr. ____ ____ a neurologist and also an "eye" man and they state that she has metastatic growth in her brain between the third and fourth nerves and that her case is hopeless.

She is suffering very severe head pains practically all the time, although there seems to be some let up at times, and some days she is apparently comfortable and other days very sick with pains and vomiting, of the violent type. She receives morphine two to three times in a 24 hour period. Her eyes appear crossed and she has double vision practically all the time. A spinal puncture was taken and the fluid tested normal only the pressure soared over 180 millimeters. At the present time her heart action and respiration is "good".

I can't believe that something cannot be done, believing that where there is life there is hope, and would appreciate hearing from you as to what your suggestion would be in her case, and anxiously await your reply.

Very truly yours,

Transcription of Letter

(A question mark is placed where the letter is illegible. Spelling has been untouched, left as is in the letter, uncorrected.)

July 1934

Dr. Fred Rankin,
Lexington, Ky.

Dear Dr. Rankin,

The writer has just spoken to Mr. Faler of this city on whom you gently performed an operation for candy, and he suggested that I communicate with you regarding my wife who has been seriously ill for the past 10 weeks. The following information will give you an outline of her trouble.

August 1932, she had her left breast removed entirely due to malignant condition, at that time. ? . . . appeared a lump at the top of her incision was also removed; however even after this second operation she complained at various times that it pained her where this lump was removed.

About ten weeks ago she was taken ill with a severe vomiting spell and pains in her head, and complained about her eyes troubling her. She was treated for about 4 weeks by a medical man for neuralgia, suffering all this time with severe pains. We then called in Dr. Leslie Asbray the surgeon who performed the operations, who in turn had Dr. Howard McIntyre a neurologist and also an "Eye" man and they state that she has metastatic growth in her brain between the third and fourth nerves and that her case is hopeless.

She is suffering very severe head pains practically all the time, although it seems to be some let up at times, and some days she is apparently comfortable and other days very sick with pains and vomiting, of the projectile type. She receives morphine two to three times in a 24 hour period. Her eyes appear crossed and she has double vision practically all the time. A spinal puncture was taken and the fluid tested normal only the pressure showed over 100 millemerers. At the present time her heart action and respirtion is "good".

I can't believe that something cannot be done, believing that where there is life there is hope, and would appreciate hearing from you as to what your suggestion would be in her case, and anxiously await your reply.

Very truly yours,
I. B. Byer

JULY
TWENTY-ONE
1 9 3 4

MR. I. B. BYER
SCHWARTZ TAILORING COMPANY
224-228 EAST 6TH STREET
CINCINNATI, OHIO

YOUR LETTER OF JULY 20 IS BEFORE ME. I DEEPLY REGRET THAT I AM UNABLE
TO GIVE YOU MUCH COMFORT OR HOPE AFTER READING OF YOUR WIFE'S CONDITION.

OBVIOUSLY THE DIAGNOSIS OF METASTATIC MALIGNANCY FOLLOWING A CANCER OF
THE BREAST REMOVED TWO YEARS AGO, CANNOT BE DISPUTED. I BELIEVE THAT YOU
HAVE HAD MOST COMPETENT ADVICE AND THAT THERE IS VERY LITTLE THAT I CAN
ADD TO WHAT HAS ALREADY BEEN TOLD YOU.

I HAVE KNOWN DR. ASBURY AND DR. MC INTYRE FOR A LONG TIME. DR. ASBURY
WAS FORMERLY ONE OF MY ASSOCIATES AT THE MAYO CLINIC AND I HAVE THE HIGHEST
RESPECT FOR HIS PROFESSIONAL OPINION, CONSEQUENTLY I BELIEVE THAT THERE
WOULD BE NO ADVANTAGE IN BRINGING YOUR WIFE TO ME. REGRETFULLY, I MUST
CONCUR IN THE OPINION THAT HER CASE IS A HOPELESS ONE.

SINCERELY YOURS

FRED W. RANKIN, M. D.
F.R/EG

Transcription of Reply Letter

410-12 Security Trust Building
Lexington, Kentucky

July Twenty-One, 1934

Mr. I. B. Byer
Schwartz Tailoring Company
223-228 East 8th Street Cincinnati, Ohio

Dear Mr. Byer,

Your letter of July 20 is before me. I deeply regret that I am unable to give you much comfort or hope after reading of your wife's condition.

Obviously, the diagnosis of metastatic malignancy following a cancer of the breast removed two years ago, cannot be disputed. I believe that you have had most competent advice and that there is very little that I can add to what has already been told you.

I have known Dr. Asbury and Dr. Mc Intyre for a long time. Dr. Asbury was formerly one of my associates at the Mayo Clinic and I have the highest respect for his professional opinion, consequently I believe that there would be no advantage in bringing your wife to me. Regretfully, I must concur in the opinion that her case is a hopeless one.

Sincerely Yours,
Fred W. Rankin, M. D.
FWR/E

My grandmother Lillian Byer died on September 23, 1934, a few months after these letters are dated. She was thirty-three years old. My dad was only seven years old at the time.

Dr. Fred Rankin was a distinguished American surgeon whose career as a clinical surgeon and a military surgeon was one of outstanding achievement. He became only the third person at that time to be elected president of three outstanding medical societies: the American Medical Association (AMA) in 1941, the American Surgical Association (ASA) in 1949, and the American College of Surgeons (ACS) in 1953.

PART VI
HONEY AND HORNETS

CHAPTER

—— 14 ——

Saving a Life

*In Judaism, the obligation to save a life in jeopardy,
is considered a major value to uphold. This
obligation applies to both an immediate threat and
a less grave danger that has the potential of
becoming serious.*[1]

When my grandmother Lillian died, my grandfather Isa (who also went by the name Bo) was very angry and questioned his religious beliefs. Dad said Bo could not grasp how something so horrendous could happen to his wife; such a kind, generous, beautiful woman and human being. It was about fifteen years before Bo stepped back into a synagogue, and reignited his Jewish spark.

My beliefs were guiding me as I made my personal decisions surrounding managing my increased for breast and ovarian cancer. Judaism places the highest value on preserving human life, and six years of religious school each Sunday instilled in me that principle.

Ultimately, I made my personal decisions to have preventive surgeries (prophylactic bilateral mastectomy [PBM] and breast reconstruction and prophylactic bilateral salpingo-oophorectomy [BSO] plus hysterectomy) based on many reasons.

EIGHTEEN REASONS

> *The number eighteen (18) is universally synonymous with the word chai. Within the Jewish faith, the word chai possesses both numerical and symbolic meaning. Chai signifies life and represents being alive.*[2]

1. I carry a *BRCA1* genetic mutation, and the science indicates I have a very high risk for cancer. I educated myself and learned that these surgeries were currently the best chance I had at *drastically* reducing my breast cancer and ovarian cancer risk. With my being a *BRCA*-positive woman, these surgeries were my best chance for "a cure."

2. There was a history of breast and ovarian cancer in my family, at ages under fifty years old.

3. I'd previously had a benign brain tumor, a very intense experience both physically and emotionally. I decided I did not want to *ever* go through an actual cancer diagnosis if I could help it. I was already having brain scans every few years. I saw a life before me of brain scans and breast scans. I did not want that to be my existence, my life.

4. I'd seen Sista on the floor with the death pain of ovarian cancer.

5. I'd watched my dear friend Kristin (also *BRCA1* positive) go through triple-negative (which is aggressive, hard to treat) breast cancer, radiation, and chemotherapy and then die at age forty-two, leaving behind her husband and young daughter.

6. The research shows that *BRCA1* carriers that get breast cancer tend to get triple-negative (difficult to treat) breast cancer. I had no interest in having triple-negative breast cancer—or any kind of breast cancer—if I could help it.

7. I had utmost confidence in my breast surgeon and plastic surgeon, both knowledgeable about *BRCA* mutations.

8. My grandmother died at thirty-three years old of breast cancer in 1934, and I had the knowledge that her fate did not have to be mine.

9. I did not want to live with constant anxiety, anticipating my next MRIs, mammograms, and ultrasounds. I didn't want to live a life of scan stress or *scanxiety*.

10. There are no reliable surveillance methods for ovarian cancer.

11. My sister was diagnosed with both uterine cancer *and* ovarian cancer. *She was later diagnosed with breast cancer.*

12. A nipple-sparing, skin-sparing bilateral mastectomy with breast reconstruction can be a one-step surgery—the nipple and skin remain intact. Breast reconstruction has come a long way. *It's just fat and tissue,* I thought. *And who needs fat and tissue if it can kill you? Let's replace that stuffing so I can live.*

13. I did not want the anxiety of constantly touching my breasts to feel for lumps.

14. I did not want to go through chemotherapy if I could help it.

15. I needed to be here for my kids.

16. I needed to be here for my husband.

17. I needed to be here for me.

18. I needed to live, to be alive, to remain breathing.

If you are of Ashkenazi Jewish descent, that alone raises an eyebrow for concern.

Approximately one out of every forty-three Jewish people carries a mutation in the *BRCA1* or *BRCA2* gene. Ashkenazi means "eastern European." Approximately 90 percent of American Jews are Ashkenazi. There are three *BRCA* mutations (two in *BRCA1*, one in *BRCA2*) frequently seen in people of Jewish ancestry. These mutations trace back thousands of years to three common ancestors in eastern Europe and have been passed down through the generations. At least one of these mutations is frequently seen in Jews who are not Ashkenazi, as well as in those who are, so it is important to focus on Jewish ancestry in general. One in forty-three American Jews carries one of the three Jewish founder mutations, as opposed to the *BRCA* frequency of approximately one in six hundred in non-Jews.

There are cancer risk ranges for *BRCA1* and *BRCA2* carriers. Unfortunately, we cannot yet narrow down exact risks based on a particular mutation or a particular person, and we cannot predict if or when a person would develop which cancer. The greatest risks for female *BRCA1* carriers are for breast and ovarian cancer, and for male *BRCA1* carriers prostate and breast cancer. The average ages of onset for these cancers tend to be younger than seen in the general population and as compared to those in *BRCA2* carriers. The greatest risks for female *BRCA2* carriers are for breast and ovarian cancer, and the greatest risks for male

BRCA2 carriers are prostate and breast cancer. And both male and female *BRCA2* carriers are at increased risk to develop pancreatic cancer. There are other cancer risks seen in *BRCA* carriers, but these are the greatest risks.
—Ellen Matloff, MS, CGC,
CEO of My Gene Counsel

CHAPTER

—— 15 ——

Prophylactic Surgeries, Drastic Reactions

*Do what you feel in your heart to be right—for
you'll be criticized anyway. You'll be damned if you
do, and damned if you don't. In the long run, we
shape our lives, and we shape ourselves. The process
never ends until we die. And the choices we make
are ultimately our own responsibility.*
—*Eleanor Roosevelt*

"Wow, that seems pretty drastic."
"Just rub this cream on your breasts, and that will prevent breast cancer."

"Your family is cursed."

"You are obviously not a spiritual person and don't believe in
God."

"Just eat more carrots."

"But *you don't know* that you *will* get cancer. You should just
have more antioxidants, up your vitamin D."

"You know, surgery is extreme, and I would never do that."

"Do you want me to be phony and pretend I support you getting yourself chopped up?"

"You know if you eat a nonalkaline diet, that keeps cancer away."

"Why would you cut off your breasts like that?"

"That seems really extreme. Why don't you just monitor yourself?"

"You know you will go through menopause, don't you?"

"Won't that dry you up if you take out your ovaries?"

"How can you feel like a woman with your woman parts gone?"

"You will get old so much sooner if you go through menopause now."

"I can't support you if you are going to cut off your breasts like that."

"Why on earth would you do that to your body?"

"Why would you mutilate yourself like that?"

The first seven comments above are actual comments/reactions I received from people when I told them about my prophylactic surgeries. A few of these comments I'd received even after I explained the science behind having a *BRCA* gene mutation and mentioned that I'd had these surgeries to drastically reduce my cancer risk.

The other comments are reactions other women have received when they told others they carried a *BRCA1* or *BRCA2* gene mutation and were going to undergo a prophylactic bilateral mastectomy or prophylactically remove their ovaries and fallopian tubes.

*Is it drastic to have prophylactic surgery, or is it that
these reactions to prophylactic surgery are drastic?*

Why such moral outrage about someone else's personal health decisions? Why such judgment, such insensitivity? Is it ignorance? Lack of knowledge about genetic mutations and *BRCA*? Malice? It must be lack of education surrounding the science and real cancer risk of *BRCA* gene mutations. It is plausible someone is just an asshole too. I mean, some people are just insensitive assholes, right?

> As a genetic counselor who has worked in the field for over eighteen years, I have been shocked, saddened, horrified, and angered by the inappropriate, inaccurate, and frankly inane comments I've heard over the years by "friends," family members, and even health care providers. However, we have made great strides in education and acceptance over the past decade, and I find fewer and fewer students are surprised when we discuss prophylactic surgeries in medical school lectures. Nonetheless, comments like the ones listed above are painful, insensitive, and very hurtful. Remember that such comments usually stem from ignorance rather than malice. If you can, you may take the opportunity to educate people who make such comments. If you cannot, remember that these decisions are yours to make about your own body and that you are supported by decades of research and like-minded individuals.
>
> It's your body and your decision, and you have no doubt made these decisions after collecting information and soul-searching the best options for you and your loved ones.
>
> These decisions are personal and private, and they belong to you. Think carefully about with whom you want to share your decisions. You do not owe anyone an explanation of why you've

made these decisions. If anyone is not supportive or dares to lash out at you, you must
decide if that person is worthy of a response.
If so, let the individual know that his or her insensitive and uninformed comments have hurt
you. If not, move on and think carefully about
whether to share information with that person
in the future.
—Ellen Matloff, MS, CGC, My Gene Counsel

More often than not in the last eight years since my surgeries,
people have been both incredibly supportive and sensitive. However,
there have been a handful of people who have reacted very insensi-
tively to my medical decisions. Today, when someone responds with
negative statements, I make an effort not to be defensive but to look
at it as an opportunity—an opportunity to educate. I try to inform the
person about how someone who has inherited a *BRCA1* or *BRCA2* gene
mutation or another hereditary cancer syndrome has a much higher
cancer risk than someone in the general population. I do my best to
be tolerant with such a person and give him or her all the exceedingly
high numbers while explaining the science. Answering questions and
having conversations helps get the information out there. Sometimes
the person gets it quickly, sometimes the person gets it a little bit, and
sometimes the person doesn't get it at all. Dr. Phil has a famous line:
"You either get it or you don't!" Some people just don't get it and will
even tell you that hereditary cancer doesn't exist.

The lottery explanation, as follows, is a tangible example that
sometimes allows others to grasp the emotional complexity surrounding having an increased risk for cancer:

What if you were told you had an 85 percent chance of winning
the lottery? You would go crazy in a good way!

Wow! How can you not win the lottery? An 85 percent chance!
That is only a 15 percent chance that you won't win the lottery!

Incredible odds! Amazing! Imagine the life you would have, what you would do with that money, what it would mean for your kids and the future generations of your family.

It sure would change your life and daily take a load off your back! You know you are going to win! *How can you not win?*

What if you were told you had as high as an 85 percent lifetime chance of getting breast cancer? You would go crazy in a bad way.

Wow, how can you not get breast cancer? An 85 percent chance! It's just a 15 percent chance that you won't get breast cancer.

Imagine what your life would be like, what you would do with that new *BRCA*-positive gene mutation status, what it would mean for your kids and the future generations of your family. It sure would change your life and daily add a heavy burden.

You know you are going to get breast cancer! *How can you not get breast cancer?*

Sometimes it can be tough explaining a *BRCA* gene mutation or hereditary cancer to someone because it can be like trying to explain to a person without kids why you can't get a two-year-old child to stop crying or screaming on an airplane. Most of us who are parents know that kids under the age of five just have an exceedingly higher risk of crying and screaming continuously on planes than the rest of the population does.

> I remember days before my prophylactic bilateral mastectomy my aunt said, "I really think this is a bit drastic. You could get run over by a bus tomorrow." I merely replied, "Yes, I could, but if I saw the bus coming, I would stand back and prevent it from hitting me."
>
> —Stefanie

> When people ask me why I did not wait to get cancer, I hope they find their answer in my blank stare.
>
> —Kelsey

Again, cancer risk-management decisions are highly intricate, highly personal, and highly patient specific. In order to make the best health care decisions for yourself, you must arm yourself with knowledge and education. In many *BRCA* families, generation after generation of family members has been affected by cancer, with many members dying at young ages. Studies have shown that cancer in the family with deaths at young ages can have a considerable impact on a person's decision to undergo preventive surgeries.[1] Ultimately, when it comes to hereditary cancer, knowledge about it can be lifesaving.

There are people every day who learn that they carry a *BRCA* gene mutation, another genetic mutation, or a genetic variant of unknown significance. Some people are living with an increased risk of certain cancers just because of their family medical history. Everyone has their personal experiences and beliefs that factor into the intensely personal and layered decision-making process of cancer risk management.

Again, what is right for one person may not be right for another. It's very important to do your own research and consult with your own medical professionals. There is no "one-size-fits-all" approach or decision, and ultimately you have to make the decisions that are right for you.

PART VII
HAMPERED HEALING GARDEN

CHAPTER

—— 16 ——

The Laundry Queen

We should all do what, in the long run,
gives us joy, even if it is only picking
grapes or sorting the laundry.
—E. B. White

Kristin's greatest hope was to have a boring day. All she wanted to do was live, not merely survive. I was keenly aware of that and was beyond grateful for mundane house chores such as doing laundry, washing dishes, and driving the minivan. Because I had been yearning for the status quo, I welcomed it with open arms.

As for laundry, well, I like it. No, I love it. It gets my adrenaline going. I have a strange fondness for colors, whites, darks, delicates, towels, bedding, sorting, picking out which detergent to use, and wondering if I should add an extra rinse. How about throwing in a cup of bleach with those whites or maybe using that stain-removal spray? Perhaps it's all the options. I love having options. They make me happy, bring me joy. I believe the "laundry gene" runs in Mom's side of the family—and that Mom, Aunt Marilyn, Sista, and I all have it. Yes, I believe we are all laundry positive.

Furthermore, I love my minivan, large, dull, functional, with automatic doors. Push a button, and voilà—the doors open. Jon still can't figure out the automatic door button, even after owning that van for more than ten years, but it doesn't matter. With my hefty dose of *BRCA* medical perspective, Jon's inability to figure out the minivan now makes me laugh instead of annoying me. I love my sweet, comical, yet mechanically inept husband and my smooth, easy-to-drive blue minivan. My minivan isn't one of a kind, but Jon most definitely is. And yes, that works for me.

However, as I was in my house collapsed on the floor at the end of my narrow hallway, unable to move, "boring" officially came to an abrupt end. All I could do was think, *Is this seriously how I am going to die, with my back to the goddamn minivan while staring at my fucking washing machine?*

On the morning of November 18, 2011, as I silently cursed the laundry machine and the minivan, I hoped that my one-of-a-kind, mechanically inept husband would save me.

I, the noncaffeinated mummy mommy, had woken up as usual that Friday morning and slowly made my way to the kitchen and the coffeepot. I was looking forward to hosting Brooke's tenth birthday party after school. I had been stuffing favor bags and prepping for the animal hunt theme party for a few weeks now. Thyroid pill, check. Effexor, check. Oops, forgot to pee. I walked back to my bathroom. *Argh, Jon is in there!* I headed down the hall to the other bathroom just off the laundry room. The kids would be running down the stairs for breakfast any second.

I was anticipating that extremely satisfying first sip of morning coffee when I started to have gas pains. *Wait, are these gas pains? OMG, what the hell is happening? Okay, I don't have time for this. I have Brooke's animal-themed birthday party to get ready for today. Shit. I have to make it t-o t-h-e cooouch. Made it. Whew!*

Moooommmm! Moommmmyyyyyyyy?" I heard Brooke and Ben as they ran down the stairs, and called for me. They found me in the office on the couch and started their a.m. chitter-chatter. "Hi, Mommy. What are you doing back here? Can you make us waffles for breakfast?"

"I want waffles."

"Ben, stop that! Brookie, no!"

I barely got the words out, but I said to Ben, "Go . . . get . . . Daddy."

Ben came back without Jon. "He's on the potty, Mommy."

I said slowly, so as not to alarm Ben, "Tell Daddy . . . e-mer . . . gen-cy."

I heard Jon's deep, grumpy morning voice. "What's going on?" he grunted, concerned but still half-asleep.

"Something's wrong," I said. "I don't feel right. My tummy."

In unison, Brooke and Ben chimed in. "Mommy, are you pregnant? Are you having another baby?" I was cognizant enough that I joined Jon in reply with an emphatic *no!*

I stayed on the office couch and had Jon get the kids to school. If I just stayed there on the couch and didn't move, I seemed okay. I thought I was beginning to feel better. *Gas pains—it just had to be terrible gas pains!* I had just started a new estradiol suppository to help me with my menopausal symptoms. Perhaps I'd had an adverse reaction. I told Jon to go ahead and do the remaining errands needed for Brooke's birthday party. I would call Dr. McKeen's office and see what they had to say.

I made my way back to the kitchen and double-checked that my cell phone was in my robe pocket. I would make my phone call after I got my coffee. The first sip was barely down before an overwhelming, indescribable, terrorizing physical pain came over me. *OMG, again! What is happening? What is going on!* I moved quickly to the bathroom. I didn't make it there. I ended up on my hallway floor. *This must be what it feels like to have death pain. My phone, it was in my pocket.* I dialed Dr. McKeen's office. Panicked, I hung up. I dialed Jon. No answer. I had to hang up. I was on the floor. I lay there, scared, unable to move.

On the hard tile floor, as I was incapacitated, my mind wandered. *Is this what Sista felt as she lay on the ground in the pain of ovarian cancer? Is this the kind of pain and agony my grandmother Lillian felt? Did she suffer? How long did she suffer? In 1934, were doctors even able to manage her pain?*

Consuming me now was this indescribable pain. *I am going to die, aren't I? Lillian, I may be seeing you soon.*

Fortunately, when I called Jon and immediately hung up, he sensed something was wrong. He came right home. He found me on the floor near the washing machine. Jon called Dr. Rimmer, and he also dialed 911. The ambulance came, and I was admitted to the hospital with lower abdominal pain. A boatload of tests and a CT scan showed nothing. "Watch and wait," Dr. Rimmer said. "You're going to get either worse or better, and that will give us useful information."

I am missing Brooke's tenth birthday and party.

In the hospital through the weekend, I would go from being fine to being in excruciating pain. My white blood cell count was normal. The pain seemed to be intermittent, and the scans were all normal; the first one was nonspecific. By Monday, day four, I had deteriorated and was diagnosed with sepsis. It was now an emergent situation, and it was clear I would need to be opened up with emergency surgery.

Although I was in and out of consciousness, I clearly heard a woman who I assumed was a nurse yelling out, "We are sending clergy back!"

What? Oh fuck, clergy. I am such a goner.

I got a glimpse of Rabbi Alon standing next to Jon, and I was just aware enough to know that gloom and doom filled what seemed to be a basement operating prep room.

They are thinking cancer. I know it. Peritoneal cancer?

Although I was in and out of consciousness, it was clear to me that everyone, including the doctors, was thinking the worst. As they wheeled me away to surgery, Dr. Rimmer whispered in my ear something like, "You may wake up with a colostomy bag," and Jon kissed me on the forehead.

Dr. Rimmer had a gynecological oncologist join in on the surgery. Subsequent CT scans showed fluid and free air in my belly. There was questionable free fluid and no masses. There was air in the peritoneal cavity, indicating something perforated, but just what was perforated was not immediately apparent. The doctors ruled out perforation in the colon and stomach, and eventually Dr. Rimmer saw a hole in my bladder. The fluid in my belly was urine. Dr. Rimmer said my bladder must have weakened with my previous surgery and finally burst. "Ruptured or perforated bladder."

I learned that bladder tears have a possibility of happening during or after gynecologic surgery. Apparently, this can happen if you have a lot of scar tissue. The doctors said I did have a lot of scar tissue. However, this tear happened almost two years (twenty-one months) after my complete hysterectomy and BSO.

I was in the hospital for two weeks. My kids came to visit me. Ben was seven years old now. As he crawled up beside me in the hospital bed, *a feeling* overwhelmed me.

Dad was seven years old when Lillian died.

Ben is seven years old. I am Lillian.

Ben is my dad. I am alive. Lillian is dead.

I hope you didn't suffer, Lillian. Was there grace in that you were maxed out on morphine and had no idea of your pain? Were you even aware of what was going on? What were you thinking? It was 1934. What did they do to keep you comfortable? Was it the "generational taboo" of cancer or the excruciating visible pain that made it so my dad was not allowed to go to the hospital to see you and crawl up in the bed beside you, his mother?

I hugged Ben very tight; I didn't want to let go.

I am alive. Lillian is dead.

Dad, motherless at seven.

Ben has a mother at seven.

Why am I so lucky again?

Why am I breathing?

I was able to have medical attention and medical options available to me that weren't available to Lillian or past generations of my family. All I can do is hope my kids and future generations of my family are laundry positive and *BRCA* gene mutation negative. Whatever their genetic status may be, I remain hopeful that there will be less invasive cancer risk-reducing options available for them in the future and that continued research *will* lead to a cure.

In the meantime, I will focus on joy and keep my life clean and simple. What's most important is Jon, Brooke, and Ben, everyone's health, and being of good character, with no toxic people and no drama creeping into my daily life.

So, I tolerate a lot less bullshit. I love boring. I love that I have nothing exciting to report. I am thrilled doing laundry. I'm more than okay with agonizing over what the hell to make for dinner.

CHAPTER

—— 17 ——

More to Sort

W*hat is it, Lillian?* Fall 2012 and there it is, the inkling that I needed to find out more about my grandmother. The feeling I had was, *Amy, you need to know more about me. Keep searching, keep researching.* I found myself compelled to go online, signing up at a genealogy site, and obsessively started searching for information about my grandmother and the rest of my father's side of the family. However, it all became way too overwhelming and time-consuming, so I realized I needed some help. Fortunately, I found out I could hire someone to do some research for me.

I had the researcher focus specifically on obtaining medical information on my dad's side of the family. The researcher looked into the siblings of my paternal grandmother, Lillian, as well as her parents, my paternal great-grandparents. It took months to start receiving information back, but once I did, I received the death certificates of six of my grandmother Lillian's siblings and her parents, my great-grandparents.

One way to record a family history is by drawing a family tree called a "pedigree." A pedigree represents family members and relationships using standardized symbols. As patients relate information about their family history, a pedigree can be drawn much quicker than recording the information in writing and allows patterns of disease to emerge as the pedigree is drawn.[1]

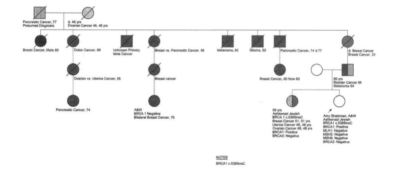

The above pedigree includes Amy and her father's side of the family. The females are represented by circles, and the males are represented by squares. Any person who has been diagnosed with a form of cancer is darkened in with a color or a symbol to represent the type of cancer diagnosis. Any circle or square with a line drawn through it indicates someone who is deceased. The numbers by each symbol represent the age of the person or, if he or she is deceased, the age at which he or she passed away.

Amy is the circle on the far right.
—Constance Murphy, ARNP, RNC, member
of the National Society of Genetic Counselors

Is this what you wanted me to find, Lillian? You wanted me to see this
map of cancer in our family? Upon seeing all the death certificates of
my grandmother's siblings, it hit me: I had not yet informed all of
my dad's adult cousins and other adult relatives about the *BRCA1*
genetic mutation in our family. I needed to do this. I had a responsibility to inform them all. After getting some advice in support
groups and looking at some hereditary cancer sites, I wrote a letter,
kept it factual and nonemotional, and sent it by regular mail, not
by email. I signed every letter and included both my phone number
and email address. I added my parents' names too so the recipients
would be sure to know who I was and how to contact me if they
had any questions.

It was also important I inform Dr. McKeen's office of this newly
found family medical history from all the death certificates. This
new family history of other types of cancers coupled with my sister's uterine cancer diagnosis, as well as some other pathology
information I'd received from family members, made the genetic
counselor at her office suspicious that an additional genetic mutation may also be going on in our family: Lynch syndrome. So, the
genetic counselor ordered a specific panel she deemed appropriate
based on this new information.

The additional genetic testing results indicated that I did not
have a mutation in one of the five Lynch syndrome genes. However,
I now had to inform my family of the possibility of another gene
mutation going on in our family. No one else in my family had
undergone genetic testing for Lynch syndrome. I gave Sista this
new information, and she decided she was not interested in further
genetic testing for Lynch syndrome.

CHAPTER

—— 18 ——

Soaking This In

The wheel is come full circle.
—William Shakespeare

Kristin underwent genetic counseling and genetic testing about one year after her initial breast cancer diagnosis and treatment. In 2012, two years after Kristin passed away, her widower, Eric, gave me her genetic testing results. To say that these are profound is an understatement. I was speechless. Of the thousands of numbered *BRCA1* mutations (or variants), Kristin and I had the same *BRCA1* mutation (variant): *BRCA1* #5385 insC, also known as #5382.

> The exact number of mutations identified on *BRCA1* and *BRCA2* is not clear. Certain labs are not sharing their mutation identification rates. There are a couple of decently sized databases that share info. I reviewed the Clinvar database. Currently the list for *BRCA1* and *BRCA2* gene

mutations [variants] reported in the ClinVar
Database is as follows:

BRCA1
Pathogenic variants listed 2580
Likely Pathogenic variants 256
Variants of Uncertain Significance 2538
Benign variants 788
Likely benign variants 1419
Variants with conflicting interpretation 325

BRCA2
Pathogenic variants listed 2992
Likely Pathogenic variants 306
Variants of Uncertain Clinical Significance
4371   Likely benign variants 2212
Benign variants 963
Variants with conflicting interpretations 571

This is based on current scientific understanding and reporting. We can certainly anticipate
changes to these numbers and interpretations
in the future.
      —Constance Murphy, ARNP, RNC, member
of the National Society of Genetic Counselors

Test Results and Interpretation   *PATIENT* (1)

POSITIVE FOR A DELETERIOUS MUTATION

Test Performed	Result	Interpretation
BRCA1 sequencing	5385insC	Deleterious
5-site rearrangement panel	No Mutation Detected	No Mutation Detected
BRCA2 sequencing	No Mutation Detected	No Mutation Detected

Analysis consists of sequencing of all translated exons and immediately adjacent intronic regions of the BRCA1 and BRCA2 genes and a test for five specific BRCA1 rearrangements.

The results of this analysis are consistent with the germline BRCA1 frameshift mutation 5385insC (also known as "5382insC"), resulting in a stop codon at amino acid position 1829 of the BRCA1 protein. Although the exact risk of breast and ovarian cancer conferred by this specific mutation has not been determined, studies of this type of mutation in high-risk families indicate that deleterious mutations in BRCA1 may confer as much as an 87% risk of breast cancer and a 44% risk of ovarian cancer by age 70 in women (Lancet 343:692-695, 1994). Mutations in BRCA1 have been reported to confer a 20% risk of a second breast cancer within five years of the first (Lancet 351:316-321, 1998), as well as a ten-fold increase in the risk of subsequent ovarian cancer (J Clin Oncol 16:2417-2425, 1998). This mutation may also confer an increased (albeit low) risk of male breast cancer (Am J Hum Genet 62:676-689, 1998), as well as some other cancers. If this individual is of Ashkenazi Jewish ancestry, it is recommended that follow-up testing of relatives of this individual include analysis for the mutations 187delAG, 5385insC and 6174delT because of reports of coexistence of two high-frequency germline mutations in some Ashkenazi families (Ramus SJ et al, Nature Genetics 15:14-15, 1997).

Kristin's BRCA test results: patient 1

Test Results and Interpretation   *PATIENT* (2)

POSITIVE FOR A DELETERIOUS MUTATION

Test Performed	Result	Interpretation
187delAG BRCA1	No Mutation Detected	No Mutation Detected
5385insC BRCA1	5385insC	Deleterious
6174delT BRCA2	No Mutation Detected	No Mutation Detected

Analysis consists of the specific mutations indicated above. The BRCA1 mutations 187delAG and 5385insC are also known as 185delAG 382insC respectively.

The results of this analysis are consistent with the germline BRCA1 frameshift mutation 5385insC (also known as "5382insC"), resulting in a stop codon at amino acid position 1829 of the BRCA1 protein. Although the exact risk of breast and ovarian cancer conferred by this specific mutation has not been determined, studies of this type of mutation in high-risk families indicate that deleterious mutations in BRCA1 may confer as much as an 87% risk of breast cancer and a 44% risk of ovarian cancer by age 70 in women (Lancet 343:692-695, 1994). Mutations in BRCA1 have been reported to confer a 20% risk of a second breast cancer within five years of the first (Lancet 351:316-321, 1998), as well as a ten-fold increase in the risk of subsequent ovarian cancer (J Clin Oncol 16:2417-2425, 1998). This mutation may also confer an increased (albeit low) risk of male breast cancer (Am J Hum Genet 62:676-689, 1998), as well as some other cancers. If this individual is of Ashkenazi Jewish ancestry, it is recommended that follow-up testing of relatives of this individual include analysis for the mutations 187delAG, 5385insC and 6174delT because of reports of coexistence of two high-frequency germline mutations in some Ashkenazi families (Ramus SJ et al, Nature Genetics 15:14-15, 1997).

Amy's BRCA test results: patient 2

Kristin is Patient 1. Amy (me) is Patient 2.

Professor Timothy Rebbeck reviewed both of the above-mentioned genetic test results without knowing they belonged to Kristin and me.

> Regarding Patient 1 and Patient 2, these two individuals have the same mutation.
> There is no way to tell based on the information that is given if Patient 1 and Patient 2 are related. However, this mutation may have arisen in a common ancestor, so the two may have common heritage.
> It is clear that this mutation is most common in individuals of eastern and central European ancestry, as this mutation arose there in the Middle Ages. They are likely to have eastern or central European ancestors and may be ethnically Jewish.
> —Timothy Rebbeck, professor of epidemiology, Harvard University

I was sure Kristin had told me she had a different *BRCA1* mutation number. I thought she mentioned that her mutation was one associated with Icelandic ancestry. What were the chances of this happening? Someone living so close to me, someone with whom I was friends, someone my husband worked side by side with, having a *BRCA1* mutation *and* the two of us having the *same BRCA1* gene mutation?

Also, how could this be since Kristin was Protestant? She was not Jewish.

How could someone who did not grow up Jewish have one of the founder mutations associated with people of Ashkenazi Jewish descent?

It is not uncommon for us to see a "Jewish" mutation in someone who is not aware that he or she is of Jewish ancestry. The most likely explanation for this finding is that that person does, in fact, have a distant Jewish ancestor. *BRCA1* and *BRCA2* mutations are present in between one in four hundred and one in eight hundred people in the general population. There are many thousands of different numbered deleterious (pathogenic) genetic mutations within *BRCA1* and *BRCA2*, and daily we are discovering new, never-seen-before mutations. There are three specific mutations deemed "founder mutations" that are associated with people of Ashkenazi Jewish descent. Approximately one in forty-three Ashkenazi Jews carries a *BRCA* mutation.

—Ellen Matloff, MS, CGC, CEO
of My Gene Counsel

What about the prevalence of *BRCA* mutations in people of other ethnic backgrounds?

There are specific *BRCA* mutations that are also more common in different ethnic backgrounds, like French Canadians, but none are as common as those found in the Jewish population. There is also a large rearrangement that is more common in Latin American populations. Contrary to popular belief, people of African ancestry can, and do, carry *BRCA* mutations. Their risk is roughly that of the non-Jewish Caucasian population. But, unfortunately, people of African

ancestry are underreferred for genetic counseling and testing, even though these women are
more likely to develop triple-negative breast
cancer—which justifies genetic counseling and
testing because *BRCA1* mutations are more
likely to be seen with triple-negative breast
cancers.

—Ellen Matloff

"Other ethnic and geographic populations around the world,
such as the Norwegian, Dutch, and Icelandic peoples, also have
a higher prevalence of specific *BRCA1* and *BRCA2* mutations. The
prevalence of *BRCA1* and *BRCA2* mutations may vary among individual racial and ethnic groups in the United States, including
African Americans, Hispanics, Asian Americans, and non-Hispanic
whites."[1]

Regarding Patient 1 and Patient 2, we would
interpret their risks to be the same, given that
all we know is the presence of a particular mutation. However, we cannot rule out the possibility that Patient 2 has other changes that were
not detected by the three-mutation panel.
Having said that, it is rare to have more than
one deleterious mutation, so in reality, the two
patients' mutational profiles are almost certainly the same.
On the test result, "Resulting in a stop codon
at amino acid position 1829 of the *BRCA1* protein" means that in the presence of this mutation, a protein is formed that is shorter than the
normal protein. This shorter protein does not
function correctly. *BRCA1* is necessary for the

normal function of cells. Because the *BRCA1* protein does not function correctly, the person is at increased risk for cancer.

The "exon" refers to the region of a gene that may ultimately get made into RNA and protein. A mutation can occur in an exon, but it can also occur in other regions of the gene that do not result in a protein.

The nucleotide designations "5385" and "5382" (different mutation numbers for the same gene mutation) reflect the fact that the numbering of nucleotides has not always been the same. For example, some groups started at one position when counting nucleotides, while other groups counted the nucleotides in a different way. A more standard nomenclature from the Human Genome Variation Society (HGVS) has a different—and more standard—way of naming the nucleotides and mutations.

— Timothy Rebbeck

Gene mutation numbers can be very confusing. Different laboratories sometimes use different numbers (also called nomenclature or terms), for the very same genetic mutation. For example, I have seen my *BRCA1* gene mutation identified as: 5385, 5382, and 5266.

CHAPTER
── 19 ──

Heavy Load

I was floored finding out that Kristin and I carried the same *BRCA1* gene mutation. Also, I was deeply affected by the death certificates that revealed a significant family history of different types of cancer in my family. Furthermore, I was frustrated by the things I had just recently come to realize but hadn't discussed with my health care providers back in 2010. For example, at the time of my BSO and hysterectomy, I had no conversation with my health care providers about fertility options such as egg freezing, in vitro fertilization (IVF), or preimplantation genetic diagnosis (PGD). Would my surgery decisions have changed if these options had been discussed? I don't know. But these options were not presented to me, and at that point, I didn't connect the dots on my own that fertility options, in general, were something a *BRCA* carrier such as myself could even consider.

Also, I realized there were no discussions *before* my BSO and hysterectomy about what to expect *after* my BSO and hysterectomy. When you have your ovaries removed, you are in immediate surgical menopause. I was now attempting to navigate life in surgical menopause, and just functioning on a daily basis and maintaining a decent energy level was a real struggle for me. Removing the ovaries before natural menopause can cause side effects and quality-of-life issues, and I was definitely experiencing some of them: weight gain, memory fog, lack of energy, lack of libido, and insomnia.

Most of my education on surgical menopause came through support groups and my own research. Not everyone has side effects after ovary removal. Everyone is different. I have consulted with many doctors and tried a multitude of drug "cocktails" to help with my variety of issues. In order to feel good, I have tried a long list of things: estradiol gel, applicator-insertable estradiol, estradiol patch, being on progesterone, being off progesterone (because I thought it made me crazy), being on testosterone, and being off testosterone (because it led to my having no sex drive). One day I went to a health food store, and the aisle attendant swore by maca root, so I tried it. Well, maca root was fine until I went to the other extreme, feeling like a combination of a dozen seventeen-year-old testosterone-driven, horny high school boys rolled into one. I tried black cohosh for hot flashes and menopause symptoms until one doctor scared the hell out of me by telling me how dangerous it could be for my liver. I have tried nighttime magnesium and calcium, melatonin, and Suntheanine formulas from the health food store to help me relax and sleep.

I "divorced" a few doctors along the way who wouldn't listen to me. I added new doctors who would listen to me. I switched from Synthroid to Armour thyroid hormone. I have been on, and I remain on, venlafaxine (the generic form of Effexor) since right after oophorectomy. I feel it helps me immensely with hot flashes and my mood. More than that, I have stayed on venlafaxine because I found that going off it is tough. When I have attempted to go off it, or if I inadvertently miss a pill, I start going through severe withdrawal. I find it helps me overall, so it is ultimately more comfortable for me to stay on it. Nonetheless, sometimes I still wake up drenched in sweat. One thing that has remained the same is that I am still officially not in a good mood until I have my morning coffee.

When you have your ovaries removed before natural menopause, it's necessary to have your bone and heart health monitored; you are at increased risk of osteoporosis (thinning of the bones) and possibly cardiovascular disease. I do have bone density scans every few years; however, I am officially overdue to see my cardiologist. I was supposed to follow up with him and have an electrocardiogram almost two years ago, but I still haven't gone. I am a human. It just gets exhausting scheduling and going to a great many different doctor appointments. Also, I still have some issues stemming from my brain surgery. Something as simple as going up and down the grocery aisle can make me downright nauseous. While I don't skip out on life, I do choose to stay home often, saying no to most activities where there will be lights or crowds.

I've done just about everything to feel and look better. I've had my vitamin levels analyzed and then custom ordered supplements to make sure I had the exact nutrition my body needed. I even bought a juicer and began juicing to help with my overall diet and energy. And, like that bread machine wedding gift, the novelty of the juicer was forgotten. When my menopausal brain remembered that I really did feel so much better after juicing, the juicer was reinstated and moved to a permanent home in clear view on my kitchen counter.

I've done no-carb, low-carb and gluten-free diets and on-again, off-again exercise—walking, spinning, and exercise videos. Also, the words depilatory and dermaplaning are now very familiar words in my vocabulary, thanks to the delightful peach fuzz that rapidly accumulates on my face, not to mention the spectacular and lovely dark and wiry Halloween witch hairs that, while thankfully don't come out of my nose, manage to sprout up again immediately after they have been removed.

Also, my dermatologist recently prescribed me spironolactone to help with the deep cysts under my skin and in my scalp. She says I will be on it for a long time. *Fantastic.* But I am here, I am alive, and this is menopausal beauty, baby.

One unexpected but enjoyable side effect of the spironolactone is that it seems to have an impact on weight loss. So, on the bright side, I'm finally back down to a size 6 from a size 10. *And you know what? I will fucking take it!*

It's been eight years since I removed my ovaries, and I am just now starting to feel like I am on the right cocktail of medicines. I feel as if I am somewhat of a rational human being. I'm not my old self, but I am functional and content. I'm a new version of my former self. The estradiol patch, .01 mg, is working for me at the moment.

I have found that I am not alone in my post–ovary removal issues. Many women I have come across have no clue what they should be doing after having their ovaries out. Many have been given no postsurgery plan and are now suffering in silence. They don't know if they should continue to have health screenings. They have depression, insomnia, weight gain, no sex drive, and quality-of-life issues.

So, what can "previvors" do?

The typical standards of medical care do not apply to *BRCA* carriers as they are often not sufficient. It's important for both female and male *BRCA* carriers to have a team of health care providers with individualized expertise. In addition, cancer risk management is not one size fits all. Many things must be taken into account when considering prophylactic surgeries and treatment for a *BRCA* mutation: your personal lifestyle, whether or not you already have children, your current physical health. What does cancer risk mean for you personally and

for your family? *BRCA* carriers need to have a
road map, a comprehensive approach to managing the *BRCA* mutation—a manager. It's the
exact reason why I started this clinic [Center
for *BRCA* Research]. For example, regarding
risk-reducing surgeries, it's crucial [that] women
consult with both a breast surgeon and a plastic
surgeon so that they may fully understand their
mastectomy / breast reconstruction options.
Prior to removing ovaries, it's important one
has a discussion with a gynecologist who has
expertise in and understands menopause
symptoms and how to minimize detrimental
effects on quality of life and overall health.
By my establishing the clinic, men and women
now have one place where they can undergo
genetic counseling, any subsequent genetic
testing, and screening for cancer, and most of
all they have a place where they can address
their individualized *BRCA*-related health care
needs and get regularly updated on the latest research and progress surrounding *BRCA*
mutations

—Pamela Munster, MD,
Professor of Medicine, Coleader,
Center for *BRCA* Research Hereditary
Cancer Clinic http://brca.ucsf.edu/

Dr. Pamela Munster herself was diagnosed with breast cancer
at age forty-eight in 2012. Although she did not have a strong family
history of cancer, she tested positive for a *BRCA2* gene mutation.
After surgery, Munster realized she would now also need a lifetime
of pancreatic screenings and screenings for skin cancer because

of her *BRCA2* mutation. As a physician who is also *BRCA* positive, Munster has unique insight into her patients.

Regarding hormone therapy use for previvors, Dr. Susan Domchek of the Basser Center for *BRCA* concludes in a 2016 study, along with coauthor Dr. Andrew Kauntiz, that hormone therapy should be considered for previvors from the start of early menopause and continue until at least the age of natural menopause. Young mutation carriers with or without intact breasts should not postpone or avoid risk-reducing (and lifesaving) bilateral salpingo-oophorectomy because of concerns that subsequent use of systemic hormone therapy will elevate breast cancer risk.[1]

All decisions surrounding managing menopause are deeply personal and highly patient specific. Communicating with doctors and speaking up for yourself is crucial.

Some helpful things to remember are as follows:

- At all doctor appointments be prepared with questions.
- Don't be afraid to ask a lot of questions.
- Have a notebook.
- Get second opinions.
- Discuss postsurgery protocol/options *before* surgery.
- Be your own advocate.
- Discuss hormone replacement therapy (HRT) and share research studies with your provider.
- Discuss the importance of quality-of-life issues.
- Discuss possible medication for hot flashes.
- Discuss insomnia.
- Do not let doctors minimize the aftereffects of having your ovaries taken out. You will be in instant menopause. Every woman is different, and no one can predict how you will feel after surgery.

Like *BRCA*, Lynch syndrome is an autosomal-dominant inherited condition. Lynch syndrome significantly increases your risk of colon cancer and various other cancers, including breast cancer, depending upon which of the five known Lynch syndrome mutations you have. When I found out I had Lynch syndrome in 2011, it was highly recommended by my certified genetic counselor and various doctors that I undergo a hysterectomy and oophorectomy to prevent malignancy to my reproductive organs. Thankfully, at forty-eight, I don't have cancer and am still here for my minor son. Little did I know that these so-called "risk-reducing surgeries" would change my life profoundly and forever.

As new data becomes available, the risk of ovarian cancer for those specifically with a MLH1 Lynch syndrome mutation has significantly decreased. If the current data were available to me in 2011, I would have chosen to keep my ovaries. It is important to speak to a certified genetic counselor to understand the slight variation of cancer risks amongst the five Ls mutations—not all Ls mutations warrant ovary removal.

I may have reduced my cancer risks through these surgeries but not without negative implications and at a significant cost. I am not the same person that I was seven years ago—physically or emotionally. Prior to surgery, I was a fit, healthy, daily runner with no health issues. Over the past seven years, I have developed

high blood pressure, high cholesterol, hypo-
thyroidism, bone loss, and brain fog and have
suffered severe depression. Some research on
women undergoing oophorectomy prior to
natural menopause validates many of my new
health challenges, showing there are serious
implications for cardiac health and cognitive
issues such as Parkinson's disease.
It has taken a constellation of factors for me to
achieve some semblance of a new normalcy
following surgery. Years of tweaking hormone
replacement therapy, psychotherapy, and
medical intervention; reading about cancer
and genetics; and finding doctors well versed
in hereditary cancer screening has helped
tremendously.

—Georgia M. Hurst, MA, Lynch syndrome previvor,
former executive director of the nonprofit
organization ihavelynchsyndrome.org, and
cocreator of #GenCSM on Twitter

Dr. Theodora Ross also has a unique perspective as both physician and patient, as she is a medical oncologist who is positive for a
BRCA1 gene mutation. In spite of her knowledge and the history of
cancer in her family, including her uncle, father, mother, brother,
and sister, Ross didn't undergo genetic testing until her diagnosis
of melanoma. Ross had a double mastectomy and had both of her
ovaries removed in 2004.

Any hormone fluctuations can cause symptoms
like hot flashes, fatigue, and emotional changes.
Our bodies work continuously to keep us on
an even hormonal footing throughout stressful

days and sleepless nights and when we've had too much food, too many drinks, or even too much exercise or too many celebrations. We obviously throw a huge monkey wrench into this system when we suddenly discard a major component of the hormonal regulatory system (our ovaries). Our bodies respond to this regulatory loss with bothersome symptoms due to the lost balance. This can also happen to us when we change our hormone replacement therapy (HRT) dosage, even if by a relatively small increment.

Once our bodies have had some time to adjust to the transition, these symptoms decrease. Symptoms are useful when adjusting to hormone replacement therapy, since these symptoms signal to us that we have, in fact, done something effective to change our hormone levels. In that way, then, transitional symptoms play a positive role in confirming that change is occurring. Transition symptoms are more accurate than monitoring blood levels of hormones. This transition time varies for women and may range from months to years.

Use of estrogen HRT is an option for *BRCA* mutation previvors as well as for some other hereditary cancer syndrome previvors who have had their ovaries, uterus, and breasts removed. The recommendation for estrogen HRT use is until the age of fifty or so. For those who have removed just the ovaries and breasts (uterus still intact), the option and recommendation is both estrogen and progesterone HRT.

Literature is continuously evolving in this area, and it's important to have a primary MD, gynecologist, or other physician managing your HRT who is up to date on the literature.

There is recent data/research indicating that a specific type of rare uterine cancer is at an increased incidence in *BRCA1* female mutation carriers. However, there has been no association for *BRCA2* mutation carriers observed. Recommendation to have a hysterectomy in addition to a BSO (bilateral salpingo-oophorectomy) is more nuanced and depends a lot on an individual's family history as well as other issues. The hysterectomy is a much bigger operation than having a BSO only. The BSO (depending on how close the woman is to achieving natural menopause) may hold significant quality of life issues for a woman. Women who are farther away from achieving natural menopause and undergo the BSO may have greater difficulty adjusting to the rapid loss of estrogen, compared to someone who is already approaching menopause. (This is not age based—not all women in their late forties are entering menopause. Please notice my wording here.)

CA-125 and vaginal ultrasound are not useful as they do not detect early ovarian cancer. In my practice, we do not recommend their use. In fact, we no longer routinely follow patients who have been diagnosed with ovarian or primary peritoneal cancer with CA-125. It leads to overtreatment and potential early death from

chemo-toxicity (http://www.thelancet.com/jour-
nals/lancet/article/PIIS0140-6736(10)61268-8/
abstract).

After ovary removal, a baseline bone density
screening is recommended. Make sure calcium
and vitamin D intake and levels are normal,
whatever the normal range is for the laboratory test.

BRCA2 mutation carriers need a baseline skin
check from a dermatologist, as do BRCA1 mutation carriers who have a family history of melanoma. If there is a family history of pancreatic
cancer, it is advisable that BRCA1 or BRCA 2
mutation carriers see a gastroenterologist at
least once and discuss having an EUS (endoscopic ultrasound). If there is colon cancer or
other cancers in the family that suggest a different genetic syndrome, a schedule for colonoscopy screening needs to be discussed with
one's physician.

Recommendations for management of patients
with BRCA mutations will change. Science is
always a set of approximations there are a
lot of myths. One of the biggest myths is that
screening saves lives for all types of cancers.
Screening has been shown to be good for tumor types that are slow growing, such as cervi-
cal cancer and colon cancer. No study has ever
claimed that because a cancer is detected by
mammography, it is, necessarily, a life saved.
Still, this has become a widespread belief.

Lots of misinformation out there.
—Theodora Ross, MD, PhD, professor of
oncology and internal medicine and director
of the Cancer Genetics Program at University
of Texas Southwestern Medical Center

PART VIII
REPURPOSED FLOWERS

CHAPTER

—— 20 ——

Angelina

"**H**ere's your champion!" Jon yelled, pushing the iPad in my face.

"*What!*" I shrieked, immediately popping out of bed upon seeing the screen. It was May 14, 2013, and Angelina Jolie had written a heartfelt and moving op-ed in *The New York Times* entitled "My Medical Choice."

> Angelina Jolie Positive for *BRCA1* Genetic Mutation Has Prophylactic Mastectomy

> I choose not to keep my story private because there are many women who do not know that they might be living under the shadow of cancer. It is my hope that they, too, will be able to get gene tested, and that if they have a high risk they, too, will know that they have strong options.[1]

> —Angelina Jolie

Us "previvors" now had a major voice. Angelina writing that op-ed and the media frenzy that followed put the acronym *BRCA* on the world's radar. Jolie was beyond articulate explaining her "medical choice." Now I could start a conversation about *BRCA* with one word: *Angelina.* The name Angelina Jolie was a gateway for me to tell my own story. In that one week, her story allowed me to secure two television interviews, two live television segments, two radio spots, and two news articles sharing my own story and explaining to everyone the nuts and bolts of *BRCA.* Jolie's op-ed had fueled my advocacy efforts, allowing me a fantastic platform to help educate others.

"I have what Angelina has."

"I did what she did."

"I, too, have a *BRCA1* gene mutation."

Through Angelina's story, most news reporters, anchors, directors, and producers were getting their first glimpse into *BRCA* gene mutations at the same time as their audience. I had seen this happen before with Kristin's story, when her local news colleagues learned of *BRCA* through her reporting.

> When Kristin was diagnosed, and when doctors confirmed [that her breast cancer] was *BRCA* related, it was a learning time for all of us. None of us in the newsroom was familiar with it. Only through Kristin's courageous reporting did we learn about it.
> —Tiffany Kenney Wiseman, friend of Kristin, news anchor

Just weeks before Angelina Jolie made her announcement, former *American Idol* judge and singer-songwriter Kara Dioguardi announced that she too had a *BRCA* gene mutation (*BRCA2*). Unfortunately, Kara's story got lost in the shuffle when Angelina Jolie came forward.

When it is Angelina Jolie, people are interested; people listen. The "Angelina effect" was named and studied in various ways by researchers following Jolie's first op-ed in *The New York Times*; studies on genetic testing showed there was a surge in demand for genetic testing.[2] I felt a big responsibility to capitalize on Jolie coming forward and share crucial hereditary cancer information and education anywhere and everywhere that would have me.

Overall, I believe Jolie's effect was positive. A global celebrity coming forward about health issues tends to get media attention. A star of epic magnitude like Angelina sharing her story gets worldwide media attention. Both of Jolie's op-ed articles have allowed stories about cancer risk-management decision-making and *BRCA* gene mutations to be told in the media, which has allowed the facts and science surrounding hereditary cancer and *BRCA* mutations to start to get out there. Because of this, Jolie has empowered women across the globe with knowledge about *BRCA* gene mutations. The knowledge that Jolie shared can be lifesaving.

> My mother died of ovarian cancer at forty-two (diagnosed at thirty-seven). My sister died of breast cancer at fifty-three (diagnosed at thirty-eight). I am forty and just had my first child. Angelina Jolie pushed me to get tested even though [previously] I knew I had to. I was scared. I tested positive for *BRCA1*.
> I will have tubes and ovaries removed and a double mastectomy. I don't know [Jolie] or even like Hollywood. But her story just made it more real for me for some reason. I [had been] in denial for a long time.
> —Lisbeth W.

When Angelina came forward with her second op-ed piece discussing her ovary removal, it was an enormous opportunity for me to spread large gold nuggets of lifesaving hereditary cancer education on an even broader platform. My phone started ringing immediately. In one week, I was interviewed for two news articles, participated in a live television web chat, held an impromptu hereditary cancer Twitter chat, and appeared on television twice, with one of those television segments being eight minutes long. I reemphasized in these interviews what Jolie said in her second op-ed, that the most important thing is to learn about the options and choose what is right for you personally.

> There is more than one way to deal with any health issue. The most important thing is to learn about the options and choose what is right for you personally.[3]
> —Angelina Jolie

By sharing that she had her ovaries, fallopian tubes, and breasts removed, Angelina Jolie has had an impact on women on so many levels, forcing us again to redefine womanhood and beauty. As a global superstar, a strong independent woman, and a humanitarian who happens to be considered one of the most beautiful in the world, Jolie was seen demystifying traditional views of femininity and challenging notions of what makes a woman attractive, empowering women to take charge of their health.

Jolie recognized the importance of discussing the cancer risk-management decision-making process and recovery. Jolie talked about consulting with various medical experts to make the best health care decisions for herself and shone some light on the aftermath of surgery: menopause and menopausal symptoms. However, whereas Jolie was able to reach out to multiple medical experts, which is highly beneficial to making decisions

surrounding cancer risk-management and postsurgery menopausal effects, many people may not have that luxury. Also, in her
op-ed articles, there was a missed opportunity to discuss hereditary cancer and men. Men who carry a *BRCA* gene mutation have
different ramifications than women, and yet they are still very
much at risk for certain cancers. However, Jolie is not an expert;
she is a patient. Did she have a responsibility to write this op-ed
with a medical expert, or did the media have a responsibility to
cover the story correctly?

When discussing ovarian cancer in her second op-ed, Angelina
mentions "elevated markers." However, Jolie did not include this
one critical statement:

There are currently no reliable screening methods for ovarian cancer.[4]

The news media overall focused on Jolie's mastectomy rather
than educating people about hereditary cancer. Rarely were the
most qualified experts (certified genetic counselors) interviewed on
television or radio, so the genetics education and awareness got lost
in the news coverage. Overall, the media focused on the glamour,
the mastectomy, and Jolie "removing her breasts."

Hereditary cancer is a very complex subject, and focusing on
the mastectomy was an attention-grabbing way for the media to
cover the story. Yes, it was a way for media to achieve great ratings.
However, I also believe media professionals did not understand
the intricacies surrounding *BRCA* or hereditary cancer to report on
the subject adequately. For example, most of the interviews I read
or saw on the news were with a physician who did not specialize
in genetics. Since Jolie's initial op-ed article was such a huge story,
a global story, it seemed to me that many news outlets, television
shows, and radio stations were just scrambling to get any medical
expert on the air (no matter the person's qualifications) as fast as
they could. Yes, I did see news media interviewing breast surgeons

about her mastectomy, but the education about *why* Angelina Jolie had a mastectomy seemed to be secondary and even tertiary in many of the interviews.

So what would have happened if a certified genetic counselor had cowritten the op-ed articles with Angelina? Hereditary cancer risk in men would have undoubtedly been part of the discussion. A certified genetic counselor would have illustrated the specific cancer risks for both female *and* male *BRCA* gene mutation carriers. *Men can also be BRCA carriers.*

However, since Jolie did not write her pieces with a certified genetic counselor, it was a missed opportunity to talk about the importance of certified genetic counseling and a missed opportunity to list resources indicating what potentially affected people can do and where they can go. For example, if after reading Jolie's op-ed, someone thought they might be at an increased risk for certain cancers, a reference included by *The New York Times* would have been most helpful. If an organization such as the National Society of Genetic Counselors (nsgc.org) had been mentioned in the op-ed, then readers would have been able to find a certified genetic counselor near them or talk to one via telephone. At the very least, it would have been great to have a sentence written by a science editor or by Jolie herself empowering women and men to advocate for themselves—that is, encouraging readers who are concerned about their own risk of cancer to discuss this concern with their doctors or ask for a referral to a certified genetic counselor. Perhaps this would have then had a trickle-down effect on how the media covered the Jolie story. News outlets might have talked more about the science and the facts and explained how hereditary cancer is very different from "sporadic" cancer.

There are many other hereditary cancer genes besides *BRCA,* many syndromes besides Hereditary Breast and Ovarian Cancer syndrome. For example, variations in the MLH1, MSH2, MSH6, PMS2, or EPCAM gene increase the risk of developing Lynch syndrome. The TP53 and CHEK2 genes are associated with Li-Fraumeni syndrome. Changes involving at least four genes, PTEN, SDHB, SDHD, and KLLN, have been identified in people with Cowden syndrome or Cowden-like syndrome. From what was "omitted" in the news coverage of Jolie's story, it's feasible that both women and men may have a false sense of security if they now go to their primary care physician or ob-gyn who is not trained in genetics and simply request "BRCA testing." If a person does this and receives a "negative" BRCA test result, it is still entirely possible that the individual holds a mutation in another gene—just another huge reason why a certified genetic counselor is vital in the genetic testing equation. Correct and thorough cancer risk assessment and accurate interpretation of genetic test results are what gives those genetic test results meaning.

Angelina Jolie definitely "started a conversation"; she planted a seed that has allowed patients to bring concerns of genetically inherited cancer risk to their doctors. She put the acronym BRCA on doctors' radar, health care providers' radar, and the world's radar. Angelina has most definitely had an impact on physicians being aware of hereditary cancer, physicians listening more closely to a patient's concerns, and patients advocating for themselves.

Jolie's openness in sharing her very personal hereditary cancer BRCA story in two op-ed pieces has only helped me empower others through advocacy. Her openness has opened the global door of communication on genetics, BRCA mutations, and hereditary cancer. Before Jolie came forward, families affected by cancer may not have even known to have these conversations about hereditary cancer risk or that such a thing as hereditary cancer even existed. Families who have swept the issue of hereditary cancer or certified genetic counseling or testing under the rug may now feel they can no longer bury their heads in the sand. Angelina sharing her story may now give families with family members who currently have cancer or who died of cancer the thought that maybe the disease in their family has a hereditary component and perhaps they need to find out more. I view all of this as a huge step forward and as progress—a very positive societal change. I often ponder that possibly if health care providers were to start a patient appointment with an initial mind-set of "hereditary until proven sporadic," then more hereditary cancer families would be identified and, subsequently, more lives would be saved.

Angelina coming forward forced me to look inward and re-examine life's most significant questions: What matters? Is it our health, our relationships, our character? Is life about being honorable, having a mission, a passion, a purpose—experiencing joy? Are we supposed to be continuously challenged and faced with conflict so that we are to be our healthiest self? What is the journey of life supposed to be? How will we handle things thrown our way? The one thing I was not expecting to gain from Angelina sharing her story was how much it was going to help me communicate with my daughter. My kids, Brooke and Ben, were only eight and five, respectively, when I had my prophylactic mastectomy, so at the time, Jon and I told them what was going on with me in an age-appropriate way. We told them that Mommy was going to the hospital for a "mommy checkup" and was going to have a few things fixed by the doctor.

As Brooke got older and started to see my advocacy work for those with *BRCA* and other hereditary syndromes firsthand, I felt it was necessary that I have another discussion with her, as I did not want to have a mother-daughter relationship where I thought I was "hiding" things. However, it was a struggle to find the right way to dive into that particular conversation. But not having any conversation was starting to cause me quite a bit of stress.

Angelina opened the door for me to have that conversation.

"What is up with that?" Brooke asked me one day while looking at the news on her computer. "Angelina Jolie, like, cut off her boobs or something?"

That was my cue.

"Well," I replied, "that is not exactly what happened. Let me explain it to you." I told Brooke to follow me and said that I'd like to explain it to her. We went into another room for privacy.

"Well," I said, "Angelina has a family history of cancer, and she didn't exactly 'cut off her boobs.' What she did is that she had her breast fat and tissue removed and then replaced with new, healthy tissue in the form of a breast implant. Imagine one of your stuffed animals getting new stuffing. It's a little more complicated than that, but basically, that's what she did. And she did this to save her life so that she could be there for her kids."

I continued, "The reason she did this is that she has a gene mutation that has an extremely high percentage/high chance of causing her breast tissue to be harmful, so Angelina wanted to get some new tissue before the tissue she was born with became harmful. I also did what Angelina did so I could also remain healthy, because I, too, have the same gene mutation."

I lifted my shirt so my twelve-year-old daughter could see my breasts and see how "normal" they looked. Brooke asked what I had been fearing she would ask: "Am I going to have to do this too?"

I knew that question might come, so I did my best to keep my composure. "Well, we don't know. Maybe. But that is something you don't have to think about now. That is for later, when you are an adult. Plus, medicine and research is advancing every day, which is great." I kept it positive and then casually said, "Let's go get some mac and cheese."

Everyone's experience with hereditary cancer is different. I am thankful for all I have yet to learn, see, and be. I am grateful for the knowledge and the choices. I appreciate every day that I can be here for Brooke and Ben. I am thankful for Lillian.

I still wake up every day trying to figure life itself out and determining how best to experience joy. Life is hard. Life is challenging.

But I am here. For me, I am achieving my goal, which is to remain breathing.

My one request to you, Angelina, is to please write op-ed article number three. I'd love for you to discuss your life after your hormones plummeted. What has been your menopausal experience, your symptoms? Have you had to adjust to any hormones, medications, etc.? Acknowledging these issues would be very helpful to so many women who have had their ovaries removed and are struggling with these postsurgery issues on a daily basis.

> I think Kristin would have had a very good reaction to Angelina speaking publicly about having a *BRCA1* gene mutation. And she would think it was good that she was helping people. I think it's good Angelina didn't stick her head in the sand about it and is talking about it. Would you rather die? I would think you would have more to live for than your hair or your breasts. The ovary thing, though—that's the tough one. Reproducing. Not having another child. I don't think Kristin thought she was a ticking time bomb at the time. Kristin knew she had cancer in her family; her focus, however, was on getting rid of cancer she had in her body. Her fear was not being able to breastfeed; [breastfeeding] was part of her vision of being a mother. Would Kristin have had a double mastectomy if she had known the future? I would hope so. I personally think it's a no-brainer.
>
> My message for other spouses: There is a need to get genetic counseling and genetic testing and to follow through to prevent cancer from coming to fruition. If you don't do your due

diligence, it's a horrible death. It is not a matter of if; it's a matter of when. You can't make
a plan without knowing. Know if cancer is in
your family. When you have a *BRCA* cancer, it's
a fight you don't want to take on. I don't think
all *BRCA* cancers turn into metastatic cancer or
are triple-negative cancer, but do you want to
take the chance?

—Eric Cecere, widower of
Kristin Hoke Cecere

CHAPTER

—— 21 ——

BRCA Responder

Once you have information that is lifesaving, it can be hard to live with yourself if you keep quiet about it. I believe that is just one reason Angelina Jolie came forward and told her story.

For me, I knew that the only way I could live with myself on a daily basis and go to sleep at night was to speak up and out, share *BRCA* resources, and offer support to others—pay it forward in some way. I felt a huge responsibility to do so and was genuinely compelled not to remain silent. People needed to know this information—this *lifesaving information.*

I am comfortable speaking in front of people, which I credit to my years of being involved in theater productions and singing publicly. Passion combined with not getting nervous makes it relatively easy for me to speak about BRCA and hereditary cancer on the radio, on television, and in news or magazine articles. My doctors and community give my phone number or email address to anyone who has questions about BRCA, genetic testing, breast cancer, or prophylactic surgeries—or to anyone who just needs to talk. I always make it clear that I can share my experience, knowledge, and resources but that I am not a certified genetic counselor. I provide one-on-one support in person or on the telephone, and I am fortunate to be part of the fantastic administration team for the largest Facebook support group for high-risk/BRCA-positive women—BRCA Sisterhood (over nine thousand members).

Flashback to my childhood home and our very seventies Fisher-Price toy–looking intercom system. It only ever seemed to work when Dad would use it. His agitated voice would always come in loud and clear. "Amy! Come eat dinner and . . . please respond!"

"Please respond!" Dad would always end any intercom conversation with "Please respond!"

As I now respond to all things BRCA, the name for me came easily: BRCA Responder.

Back in 2013 after the hype surrounding Angelina Jolie's announcement ran its course, I was frustrated, feeling there were still such huge voids in the BRCA and hereditary cancer community. What about the men? Why wasn't anyone stressing the importance of genetic counseling? Dots weren't connecting. There was so much that needed to be addressed in the hereditary cancer conversation.

In one day, with her first op-ed, Angelina got the world's attention. She did in one day what I could only hope to do in one lifetime. I most definitely was not Angelina. *There must, however, be some way,* I thought, *that I can reach people on a bigger scale.* I knew it was paramount to stress the importance of male cancer risk and male

BRCA carriers. I had to cast a wider net on *BRCA* education. I wanted people to pay attention, I wanted to get men to pay attention, and I wanted to paint a visual picture of what *BRCA* looks like and how it feels. I was passionate to get hereditary cancer on people's radar and give them resources and tools.

I wanted to save lives. I needed to save lives. I had to save lives.

It was about this time that I came across a post on a friend's Facebook page that said "Pink & Blue." It caught my attention. I read the post and found out that a guy named Alan Blassberg was making a breast cancer documentary. Alan was a male *BRCA2* carrier. A movie. *That's it.*

I reached out to Alan.

Alan first thought about making a documentary dealing with the realm of cancer after losing his aunt to ovarian cancer in 1998. Thirteen years later, Sammy, Alan's sister, who was *BRCA2* positive, died from metastatic triple-negative breast cancer on February 24, 2011. At the same time, his fiancée Stephanie had her breast cancer return, and his other sister, Lisa, underwent a prophylactic double mastectomy. Alan now knew it was the time for a film.

> I had no idea that men could carry a *BRCA* mutation until my sister Lisa's oncological surgeon educated me. Being surrounded by cancer, I finally decided to undergo genetic testing and discovered I, too, was also positive for a *BRCA2* gene mutation.
>
> —Alan M. Blassberg, director and producer,
> *Pink & Blue: Colors of Hereditary Cancer*

It was an instant feeling that this movie and with Alan was where I was supposed to land. Alan and I talked for hours at a time, sharing stories of cancer in our families due to *BRCA*. We both felt as if we had known each other forever. There was never a weird silent moment. Alan told me all about his sister Sammy, and I told him all about Sista. We bonded over the striking similarities in personality between them.

> Energy has a way of bringing people together. My sister Sammy was always a bright light to people around her. If she wasn't wearing an outfit that was sparkling like the sun, then she was having an off day. Sammy encompassed passion and energy I had never seen. She was indeed an original—both fun and embarrassing to witness at times. She was spiritual and was acutely aware of "life signs" the universe sent her way. Sammy would always tell me about her intuition or serendipitous things happening. I will never forget the feeling that overcame me when I first met "Sista," Amy's sister, Jan. The moment I saw her, I welled up with emotion. I had chills racing up and down my spine, and the hair on my arms was sticking straight up. Jan embodied everything Sammy. No one has ever come close to having Sammy's qualities. But Jan did. From her fabulous outfit to her adventurous stories, to the way she talked, I was thoroughly overwhelmed. I called Amy from lunch and tried to explain what I was feeling, but it was impossible. This energy made me feel like the universe had put Amy and me together to make this film. We were doing what we were supposed to be doing.
>
> —Alan M. Blassberg

Alan and I shared the same nutty sense of humor, a mutual love of dogs, and ultimately the same vision for *Pink & Blue*; we were on the same page. Our goal with the film was to get breast cancer education out there and focus on *BRCA* education in a nonthreatening way, sharing different experiences, different journeys. It was also vital for us to bring men and hereditary cancer, men and breast cancer, into the public conversation. I don't think either of us slept for about two years while making the film. The production continued to be fluid, with no significant problems through the editing process. Everything found its place and fit accordingly.

Pink & Blue: Colors of Hereditary Cancer premiered in Los Angeles and in New York's Times Square in October 2015. The film has had critical acclaim throughout the United States, Canada, and England; has won several film festival awards; and has qualified for Oscars in two categories. We continue to have screenings around the world, which usually include a Q&A panel following the film. While the accolades are excellent, the best reward for Alan and me is getting immediate feedback from people right after they have seen the film. Seeing how the film sparks conversation and spurs people to take action with their health continues to fuel my passion for advocacy and education.

Following are things that people have said to me after seeing the film:

- "You made me think about my family history."
- "I am going to contact a certified genetic counselor tomorrow."
- "I had *no idea* that men could get breast cancer!"
- "Thank you; I learned so much."
- "Very well done and very informative."
- "I want my brothers to see this film!"

My sister Sammy called me "Bertie." When someone tells me that they underwent genetic

counseling or genetic testing because of the
film, or "you saved my life," the emotions are
overpowering, and I feel the chills from the uni-
verse. I feel Sammy right there saying, "Way to
go, Bertie!"

—Alan M. Blassberg

Social media is an exciting part of advocacy. Sites such as
Twitter, Facebook, and Instagram create an incredible opportunity
to reach people in real time. Hereditary cancer resources, information, and support can be given immediately, at any time of day.

Social media and "responding" has also allowed me to connect with others who share my interest and passion for education
surrounding *BRCA* and hereditary cancer. These are people whom
I now call friends whom I would not have met otherwise. Each of
us has different experiences and insight, however, we are all united
in our dedication to supporting others and providing *BRCA* and
hereditary cancer education. We all are united in knowing that this
information can save lives.

Eight years ago I underwent genetic counseling and genetic testing and found out I carried
a *BRCA2* gene mutation. I wanted to publicly
share my experience and be a voice for others in
a similar situation. In addition, when I couldn't find
the support I needed, I started my own support
group. Alongside my friend Teri Smieja, I created the *BRCA* Sisterhood group on Facebook
to provide support for women who felt alone.
Now, seven years later, the *BRCA* Sisterhood is
the largest support group in the world. Every day
I receive messages from women who are grateful

to have a place to share their feelings with others who "get" what they are going through.

Hereditary cancer/*BRCA* advocacy has allowed me to help others by educating them about available mastectomy and reconstruction options. It was important to me to show women that you can feel beautiful after having a mastectomy and define beauty on your own terms. My personal choice was to cover my mastectomy scars with a beautiful tattoo. I want others to know that support is available to them as they navigate their own decisions surrounding hereditary cancer/*BRCA*.

—Karen Malkin Lazarovitz, *BRCA2*
mutation carrier, founder of *BRCA*
Sisterhood support group and *BRCA*
Chat Montreal support group

Advocating for women and men affected by hereditary breast and ovarian cancers is an unwavering passion of mine. It's gutsy, requiring steadfast determination and compassion. I have a deep, relentless desire to find answers surrounding *BRCA* gene mutations. Empowering myself with knowledge has allowed me to make very informed decisions about my own cancer risk reduction. If you are at high risk for certain cancers, it's important to become your own advocate. Educating yourself and following the research is one of the best things you can do

for yourself. Along the way, you may save lives
of those you love.

—Lisa M Guzzardi, RN, founder and
curator of *BRCA* Advanced 101 and
102 Journal Club via Facebook

PART IX

GARDENERS

CHAPTER

—— 22 ——

Doctor, Doctor

This doesn't make sense. Gilda didn't have to die.
I was ignorant, Gilda was ignorant—the doctors
were ignorant.[1]
—Gene Wilder

Gene Wilder was speaking out about learning from the past and family medical history not long after Dr. Mary-Claire King discovered *BRCA1*.

"We have to learn from the past," Gene Wilder said of Gilda's illness and the tragic misdiagnosis that led, he contends, to her unnecessarily early death. In 1991, Gene Wilder penned a personal essay in *People* magazine about Gilda Radner's painful death and why he believed it could have been avoided. In it, Wilder, after months of research and correspondence with cancer experts across the country, contends that Gilda didn't have to die.

Also in 1991, Wilder testified before a congressional committee to tell them just this. He said to them that Radner's condition had been misdiagnosed and that if doctors had inquired more deeply

into her family background, they would have learned that her
grandmother, aunt, and cousin had all died of ovarian cancer, and
therefore they might have attacked the disease earlier.

> All these months we'd been seeing different
> doctors. A gynecologist in California did a pel-
> vic examination and said everything was fine.
> One of the doctors thought the symptoms just
> had to do with her ovulating. In New York, her
> gynecologist said she thought it was a stom-
> ach problem. We went to a gastroenterologist
> who did some blood work, a sonogram and a
> pelvic. He said it wasn't anything life-threaten-
> ing. He said, "She's a very nervous, emotional
> girl. She's got to relax." Gilda kept saying to
> all the doctors, "It's not cancer, is it?" Every
> doctor for ten months noted that Gilda was a
> high-strung person and kept telling her, "No,
> don't worry. Go home and relax." One doctor
> told her she was literally "full of shit" and gave
> her laxatives.[2]

When Gilda first became sick, doctors diagnosed her symptoms
as Epstein-Barr virus. However, Gilda knew something was very
wrong and repeatedly told doctors she was afraid she had cancer.

> She could be alive today if I knew then what I
> know now. Gilda might have been caught at
> a less-advanced stage if two things had been
> done: if she had been given a CA-125 blood
> test as soon as she described her symptoms
> to the doctors instead of 10 months later, and
> if the doctors had known the significance of

asking her about her family's history of ovarian cancer. But they didn't. So Gilda went through the tortures of the damned and at the end, I felt robbed.

All along I kept hearing Gilda saying, "Don't just sit there, dummy, do something!"

The doctors who worked with Gilda were mostly wonderful people. But here's the thing: None of them put it all together and said, "Wait a minute, now. Does anyone in your family have ovarian cancer?" So many of the doctors wrote off what Gilda was telling them by saying she was a high-strung, emotional, nervous girl. I kept hearing Gilda shouting, "It's too late for me. Don't let it happen to anyone else.[3]

When Mom's best friend Norene "got" breast cancer, she was thirty-four, but she wasn't diagnosed until age thirty-five. Her first doctor pooh-poohed the lump in her breast, telling her she had lumpy breasts and suggested she go home and eat more protein. So, when she went back at age thirty-five and the cancer had spread to her lymph nodes, doctors told her she had five years to live. Norene died exactly five years later.

Many things were so different back then (almost forty years ago). Cancer treatment was barbaric, but for everything my mom went through I never remember her complaining. She had two separate mastectomies, a hysterectomy, brain surgery, and a whole host of treatments during her five years that she lived with cancer.

My mom was beautiful, witty, strong, and authentic. The most important thing about my mom's story is that she was thirty-four when diagnosed. The doctors felt she was too young for breast cancer when she felt her first lump. Had they taken a closer look, who knows what could have happened? In any event, women need to be very careful and begin being very familiar with any changes in their breasts at a young age. In my opinion, a first mammogram at forty-five or fifty years old is way too late.

—Valerie, Norene's daughter

CHAPTER

— 23 —

Genetic Counseling and Genetic Testing

Because genetic counseling and genetic testing are
so often linked, it can be confusing to understand
how they are different.[1]
—National Society of Genetic Counselors

How could Gilda and Norene's doctors not listen to them? How could their symptoms be overlooked? Why weren't the puzzle pieces being put together? Have things changed?

When Sista was first diagnosed with both ovarian cancer and uterine cancer, she did inquire about genetic testing during one of her initial hospital checkups after surgery. She knew there were some breast cancers on our dad's side of the family, but no one at the hospital made an in-depth inquiry about her family history. She asked one of the residents (the doctor's assistant) about genetic testing—not her doctor directly. The resident did not advise her to get genetic testing at that time. Sista had a lot going on, as she was still going through chemo for ovarian cancer, having just had a complete hysterectomy, so she did not push for genetic testing.

Sista is the one who sought out genetic counseling and subsequent genetic testing based on the ovarian cancer conference she attended in 2009.

How is it that Sista's health care providers did not initially recommend certified genetic counseling or genetic testing, considering her glaring red flags for carrying a BRCA mutation? Dr. Mary-Claire King had discovered BRCA1 eighteen years before Sista's 2008 diagnosis. Clinical genetic testing for BRCA1 and BRCA2 began in the mid-1990s. How, in 2008, could health care providers be so unaware?

I asked my gynecological oncologist Dr. Howard Goodman how this could happen. Following is his reply:

> The physicians and other providers might not have been aware of the importance of the BRCA gene and the probability of it being abnormal in an Ashkenazi female with ovarian cancer in this age group. It is hard to imagine that any physicians treating ovarian cancer are not aware of this issue.
>
> The physicians or other providers each felt that someone else would address this issue; hence, no one took the time to review [the case] and either provide genetic counseling or refer to a counselor.
>
> The involved health care providers were so busy focusing on the acute cancer problems that they did not take the time to consider the other issues, for example, possible gene abnormalities and family history.
>
> I still see this story repeating itself, with patients with incredible family histories that are screaming BRCA or Lynch syndrome, and none

of the other doctors involved in the care of that
patient have suggested genetic testing.
As I said, none of the answers are comforting.
—Howard M. Goodman, MD, Board
Certified Obstetrics and Gynecology,
Board Certified Gynecologic Oncology

I talk to many people after they receive genetic testing results.
Unfortunately, many of those people have had genetic testing without any pretest or posttest certified genetic counseling. So, I end up
becoming part therapist, part advocate, and a big connector of the
dots for them—calming them down and helping them get a certified genetic counselor to talk to in person or by telephone.

Most recently, I talked to a woman who'd been sent her *BRCA*
genetic test result directly to her house by the genetic testing lab
that did the testing, and that test result paper indicated she was
positive for a *BRCA2* gene mutation. Her ordering physician also
received her *BRCA* genetic test result at the office from the genetic
testing lab, except this test result paper indicated she *did not* have a
BRCA2 mutation or any other genetic mutation. One positive test
result for a *BRCA2* gene mutation, one negative *BRCA* genetic test
result for the same woman. I connected the woman to a certified
genetic counselor right away to help her sort out this massive genetic testing mess.

I met sisters Jessica and Stacy through my advocacy efforts.
Their story always stays in the forefront of my mind, and I cringe
when I think about how many other stories like this are out there.
How many other people out there, whom I don't know, are having
their genetic tests misinterpreted?

My sister Stacy went to her ob-gyn, and during
her visit he suggested that she take the *BRCA*
gene test. She really didn't know anything about

the test, but because her doctor suggested it, she took it. Two weeks later she went to get her results. Her doctor told her she was negative, that she had nothing to worry about, and that there was no chance of passing the gene on to her children. Stacy gave me the envelope that contained her genetic testing results, and I took it with me to my meeting with my genetic counselor. I told my genetic counselor that my sister Stacy was *BRCA* negative.

My genetic counselor asked to see the actual paper with Stacy's genetic test results. Her mouth dropped. So did mine. We were both shocked. Stacy's ob-gyn had misread her *BRCA* test results. The genetic counselor and I both looked at the paper. It read, *"Positive for a deleterious mutation."* How could Stacy's doctor have read this test wrong? How could this happen?

—Jessica

Stacy received her accurate genetic testing results through her sister Jessica's genetic counselor, who confirmed that she did indeed carry a *BRCA1* genetic mutation. Stacy then planned a preventive removal of her ovaries and fallopian tubes, a bilateral salpingo-oophorectomy (BSO). When the pathology report from that prophylactic surgery came back, it revealed that Stacy already had ovarian cancer. Stacy had chemotherapy, but her cancer returned. She passed away in 2015.

The US Preventive Services Task Force recommends that primary care providers screen unaffected women who have a family history of *BRCA*-mutation-associated cancers but who do not have a personal history of *BRCA*-related cancer for referral to genetic counseling and potential genetic testing. According to the latest research, despite this decade-old US Preventive Services Task Force recommendation, few unaffected women at risk for *BRCA*-associated cancer report discussing genetic testing with a provider.[2]

> Even though breast cancer struck several women in Kristin's family, including her mother, Kristin was always healthy and remained optimistic about her future. I don't believe she ever really thought breast cancer was something she would have to deal with, despite her family history. Back then, getting genetic testing was not something most people did. She knew breast cancer ran in her family, so why get a test?
> —Tiffany Kenney Wiseman, friend of Kristin, news anchor

Through my advocacy efforts, I continue to hear many first-hand examples pertaining to this lack of discussion surrounding genetic testing. There are primary care physicians and other doctors who are not acknowledging patients' concerns about having an increased risk for cancer. Patients are indicating that they ask primary physicians about genetic testing and that their providers tell them, "You don't need to worry about it."

On the other hand, there are many primary physicians, ob-gyns, and other doctors currently offering genetic testing in their offices. At first glance, physicians providing these tests seem smart, logical, and highly supportive of women and men and their health. However, these clinicians do not have advanced training in genetics. For that reason, I believe it is an ethical slippery slope. There are critical health decisions made on genetic test results alone. It's necessary that the genetic tests ordered are the correct ones but, even more than that, that genetic test results be interpreted correctly.

What is missing in these particular genetic testing scenarios is certified genetic counseling.

> **Genetic Counseling** is a conversation. Genetic counseling helps determine if genetic testing might be right for you—and if so, which genetic tests—and explains what results might mean for you and your family. There is a review of your medical history and understanding inherited risks. Health care and support options to consider are discussed based on possible test results. After any genetic testing, a genetic counselor will share any genetic testing results with you and your doctor and then provide support as you make informed choices. Genetic counselors have advanced training in medical genetics and counseling to guide and support patients seeking more information about how inherited diseases and conditions might affect them or their families and to interpret test results.

> **Genetic Testing** involves analyzing a person's DNA usually by taking a blood sample, though other sample collection options exist. There are thousands of genetic tests, meaning tests are available for many genetic mutations. But there are also many mutations for which there are no tests. Whether or not to have genetic testing is complicated. What will it tell you? What will you do about it once you get the results? Will having that information help you or not? That's why the insight and guidance provided by a genetic counselor are invaluable.

A genetic counselor can explain the different types of tests available and what they may— and may not—tell you as well as how they may or may not help you.[3]
—National Society of Genetic Counselors

There are many lists available that provide the names of available genetic counselors. There are also many people who call themselves genetic counselors or act like genetic counselors but are not certified and do not have advanced training in medical genetics or counseling. Not all genetic counselors and genetic counselor lists out there are created equal. I refer people to the National Society of Genetic Counselors (www.nsgc.org). Once there, click on the blue icon "Find a Genetic Counselor" and from there, you can choose "In Person" or "By Phone." *If there is not a certified genetic counselor near you, then you may speak with one by telephone.* Type in your state or zip code and under "Types of Specialization" highlight "cancer" and hit search. If you are having any difficulty finding a certified genetic counselor, please contact NSGC or me directly on social media through Twitter or my Facebook page. I will personally help you find one! To avoid test misinterpretation, speak to a certified genetic counselor *before and after* any genetic testing.

As with any other medical illness, a specialist, a certified genetic counselor, can evaluate a patient, determine his or her cancer risk from the best available knowledge, and decide whether or not he or she should proceed to the next step of genetic testing. If you think about it, for a heart problem you go to a cardiologist, and for brain issues you go to a neurologist. Why for a possible genetic defect would the need for a specialist be any different? Primary care doctors are not routinely implementing or trained in evidence-based decision-making for genetic testing or counseling. Neither are they trained nor do they have the time to assess a patient's genetically linked risk for cancer accurately. It is not their area of expertise.

Genetic counselors are translators of complex medical information. Having genetic counseling does not mean one has to undergo genetic testing. Most insurance companies have criteria for genetic testing, and certified genetic counselors have the most up-to-date information regarding whether or not the procedure will be covered by health insurance. They are also the most familiar with the most trustworthy labs for genetic testing. Even more than that, while there are discrimination laws in place (e.g., GINA), a certified genetic counselor is most familiar with the loopholes and has the ability to counsel you on the importance of obtaining life insurance *before* undergoing any genetic testing.

A certified genetic counselor knows how to interpret the genetic test results, which is hugely important since you will be making health decisions based on genetic testing results. There are over fifty hereditary cancer syndromes according to the National Cancer Institute. Also, there are many different genetic testing panels on the market. More than this, if any genetic testing you have undergone does not find a genetic mutation, a certified genetic counselor will still be able to correctly counsel you on your lifetime cancer risk and health screenings and make appropriate referrals for your monitoring and health screenings. Someone who tests negative for a gene mutation or has a VUS (variant of unknown significance) may still have a family history of cancer. Family history alone can increase cancer risk, placing someone at a higher risk for cancer than the general population. A certified genetic counselor is the most qualified individual to handle these nuances of gene testing.

> Genetic testing is not a black-and-white test the way a pregnancy test is. There are multiple tests available that look for mutations within the genes *BRCA1* and *BRCA2* (full sequencing, deletion/duplication analysis,

familial mutation testing, ethnic testing), as well as other tests that include as many as twenty-five or thirty other genes that are involved in cancer development. For this reason, it is important to see a certified genetic counselor before you have genetic testing to ensure that (a) you are a good candidate for testing, (b) you understand the risks, benefits, and limitations, (c) you get as much coverage from your insurance company as possible for the testing, and (d) the correct test is ordered. Genetic counseling is equally important after testing to ensure that (a) your test results are interpreted correctly (misinterpretation is a common and serious problem), (b) you are counseled about the surveillance and risk-reduction options that are most appropriate for you, and (c) you are given accurate information about the risks and options for your family members. If you do not have local or timely access to a certified genetic counselor, there are also counseling options available by phone or Skype.

There is an important, and frequent, misconception that only people who are found to carry a mutation require genetic counseling. In fact, people with a strong personal or family history of cancer who test negative on genetic testing often have the most challenging result interpretations and need excellent genetic

counseling to guide further testing and/or sur-
veillance and risk-reduction plans.
—Ellen Matloff, MS, CGC,
CEO of My Gene Counsel

In June of 2013, shortly after Angelina Jolie's initial op-ed article, the Supreme Court of the United States ruled unanimously
that human genes may not be patented.[4] This decision allowed
competition in the genetic testing marketplace and drove down the
cost of genetic testing. Unfortunately, there are direct-to-consumer
genetic testing kits sold without any mandatory requirements for
genetic counseling, and there are many physicians not trained in
genetics offering genetic testing in their offices. From what I have
personally witnessed, it is my firm belief that undergoing genetic
testing without certified genetic counseling is not in the best interests of your health or in your best interests, period.

As to why so many patients aren't connecting
with genetic counselors, Ellen T. Matloff, CEO
of My Gene Counsel, and the founder and former director of Yale Cancer Genetic Counseling
program, said some genetic testing companies
are partially to blame because they market testing directly to doctors, telling them they don't
need genetic counselors. "Some of these sales
reps are telling doctors, not only do they not
need genetic counselors, but we have a kit that
can help any Tom, Dick or Harry order the test
themselves."[5]

Know your family medical history. If you don't know it, start
asking questions now. The best first step someone can take toward
documenting family medical history is to write everything down

with as much detail as possible. Fill in any gaps in family medical history by reaching out to relatives by phone or email. Use
family gatherings and holidays, such as family reunions, Easter,
Thanksgiving, and Hanukkah, to ask relatives about other relatives you may have never met, any relatives who died young, or
any relatives who were sick in any way. By asking "out of the box"
questions instead of just "Who had cancer?" you may better trigger
people's memories. It is essential to write down everything health
related and not edit anything out while you are writing—even if
you think the information doesn't apply. Let the certified genetic
counselor, the expert, decipher it.

> Accurate family histories are incredibly im-
> portant [when it comes to] to guiding fami-
> lies through genetic testing and cancer risk
> assessment. When someone calls our cancer
> genetics center, we send them a "genetics
> packet" to fill out. This is a detailed personal
> and family medical history. Once we receive
> the packet and a prescription from the patient's
> health care provider, the patient is offered an
> appointment to see me in consultation for
> cancer risk assessment and genetic testing, as
> appropriate. Genetic test results are provided
> in person at a subsequent appointment. I see
> every high-risk patient, whether or not they test
> positive for a genetic mutation, annually for an
> updated care plan and to provide information
> about enhanced surveillance and risk-reduc-
> ing strategies, including surgery. The genetics
> landscape is changing rapidly. We are learn-
> ing more about the newer emerging genes.
> Therefore, it is important to have continued

contact with your genetic counselor, as it is essential to providing medically appropriate care.
—Constance Murphy, ARNP, RNC, Member
of the National Society of Genetic Counselors

Discussing family medical history and cancer with family can
sometimes be tricky. Sometimes family members do not want to
talk about anything health related or talk about genetic testing. It
can be a sensitive or taboo subject for some. Some people may say
they don't want to know. Adults have the right to make choices
for themselves. Maybe some people don't believe genetic testing
knowledge for them is power. All you can do is voice your concerns.

The same therapist who counseled me before my ovary removal suggested to me that just because a family member has
closed the door on talking about cancer risk for now, that does not
mean the door cannot be opened in the future. Everyone is in a
different place to receive cancer risk information or talk about it.
You can always revisit a conversation six months from now, a year
from now, or at some other time in the future. Maybe with some
additional education on hereditary cancer and some time, adult
family members will come around. However, some adult family
members may not ever come around or be open to conversation
about cancer risk. In my experience, it is a bad idea to beat yourself
up over what is ultimately their choice. You can only do what you
can do. It's important to focus on yourself, your health, and do what
is right for you.

Listen to your inner voice, your feelings. If you suspect that
your genes may be putting you at risk for cancer, it is ideal to discuss
your concerns with a certified genetic counselor. It's your right to
press your doctor to refer you to one. It's your right to seek one out
on your own. Be your own advocate.

Someone who agrees with the importance of genetic counseling is Dr. Allison W. Kurian from Stanford University School of

Medicine. She feels it's important that genetic tests be ordered and interpreted by genetic counseling experts. One of her recent studies, for which she was the lead author, found that breast surgeons were treating patients with variants of unknown significance the same way they were treating *BRCA*-positive patients. To summarize, Kurian says, "VUS [variants of unknown significance] should not be treated in the same way as harmful mutations. The finding raises concern that misunderstanding of VUS (believing that they cause high cancer risk when they do not) may be responsible for unnecessary bilateral mastectomies."[6]

> I have authored three case studies on genetic test misinterpretation, and a fourth is under way. The field of genetic testing is growing quickly, and the average clinician simply cannot keep up. More and more genes are being added to testing panels, making genetic test interpretation more complex. Also, there are some "gray zone" findings, called variants of uncertain significance (VUS). These can either be benign or disease-causing. When a genetic test comes back with a VUS, the interpretation and counseling are complex. In addition, VUS classifications can change over time. This represents a great challenge for the vast majority of clinicians who do not specialize in genomics.
>
> —Ellen Matloff

I encourage all physicians and all patients to understand that it's in the best interests of a patient to have the most qualified person assess and interpret cancer risk (including patients who receive a cancer diagnosis or are cancer survivors). If you are concerned about *BRCA* mutations or hereditary cancer, speak to a certified genetic counselor for correct and thorough cancer risk assessment.

Some treatment decisions can be impacted by genetic testing results, so results may be needed quickly. In my experience, there is no shortage of certified genetic counselors. They are underutilized. Not everyone needs a certified genetic counselor at the same time. Telegenetics—certified genetic counseling by phone—is an option.[7] Studies have proven that it is as effective as in-person genetic counseling. Physicians, by establishing relationships with certified telephone genetic counselors, you can fluidly integrate them into your practice. Patients, you can advocate for yourselves and request that your doctor contact a certified genetic counselor for you, or else contact one yourself.

Patients may very well be at high risk for certain cancers because of a genetic mutation, family history, or other factor with which a primary physician or other physician is not familiar or that a primary physician is not trained to decipher. Certified genetic counselors are available by telephone or in person. You can speak to one within a reasonable amount of time.

PART X
BUTTERFLIES AND BLOOMS

CHAPTER

—— 24 ——

Surprise Lily

There is one friend in the life of each of us who
seems not a separate person, however dear and
beloved, but an expansion, an interpretation, of
one's self, the very meaning of one's soul.
—Edith Wharton

Life was getting back to what Kristin wished life would be: boring. It was 2014. I was happy, and I was here. I was thankful. My experiences had forever changed my perspective. I realized what truly mattered in life is one's health, being of good character—a good person—and one's relationships.

However, I also realized that it was only a matter of time before someone else I knew would get a diagnosis of breast cancer, the statistics being that one in eight women will get breast cancer. While 10–15 percent of breast cancers are hereditary, about 90 percent of breast cancers remain sporadic. For the sporadic group, 65 percent of breast cancers are sporadic, and 20–30 percent of the cases are made up of familial cancer (familial cancer is defined differently than hereditary cancer—familial cancer is defined as those individuals who have a family history of cancer but for whom a genetic mutation has not been identified). Sporadic cancer is cancer that occurs in people who do not have a family history of that cancer or an inherited change in their DNA that would increase their risk for that cancer.

I realized hearing about a new breast cancer diagnosis was inevitable. But nothing prepared me for the following . . .

My phone rang.

The person who had been diagnosed with breast cancer was Char, my best friend.

I wanted to throw up.

> I waited a day before calling my BFF of thirty-plus years to share the news with her. I felt like such a disappointment for some reason. Amy had already been through so much herself, after testing positive for a *BRCA1* gene mutation, her sister's diagnosis, and her own courageous decisions to have a preventative double mastectomy, oophorectomy, and hysterectomy. She had taught me so much about "owning" my health, but what she went through had me in awe. I remember calling her and just crying. She asked me questions I just couldn't answer. All I knew was that I was diagnosed with stage 0 DCIS, and in my mind, if you're going to get cancer, stage 0 sounds pretty darn awesome.
>
> —Char

I'd quickly befriended Char, the new brown-eyed, brown-haired fifth grader with a cast on her arm. Ours was an instant friendship of passing origami notes, playing soccer, and making our parents crazy with our made-up "baby talk" language while wearing matching rainbow hair ties.

"Hi. Wanna sit next to me? Where are you from? Wanna play Chinese jacks? Can you sleep over?"

"OMG, he totally likes you."

"No he doesn't."

"Yes, he does."

When Char moved to another state in seventh grade, it was the first time in my life I felt a significant loss and severe emotional suffering. Dad was very concerned about me at the time and said, "Amy, you'd better make some other friends."

I did make other friends, but the friendship that began on the playground in fifth grade survived and has thrived for thirty-nine years, through moves, cross-country colleges, heartthrobs and heartbreaks, brain tumors, breast cancer, weddings, marriages, in-laws, kids, nonstop laughter, losing loved ones, first homes, divorce, and vats and vats of Rice Krispies treats.

Char: forty-five years old, in excellent health, a hardworking mother of two, an avid cross-fitter, and a weekend runner. She traveled a lot for her job and endured high stress and anxiety on an almost daily basis, but exercising was her relief. She was fortunate to work for a company that encourages annual physicals, including mammograms, so in August of 2013 she went in for her yearly mammogram, not realizing that she had skipped it in 2012. After her images were taken, the radiologist wanted to see Char to show her a tiny white fleck on the image of her right breast. "Not to worry," the radiologist assured Char, "you have dense breast tissue, but we should keep an eye on it and recheck it in six months." So, Char thought nothing of it.

Seven months later, Char realized she had forgotten to have that little fleck checked, so she went back to the clinic and had her mammogram. That small white fleck appeared. "Still no cause to worry," the radiologist assured Char. "It's no bigger than before, but it looks a little different, so you should probably have it checked by your doctor." Again, Char thought nothing of it. To her it seemed like an accidental speck of dust on the screen.

> Breast cancer does not run in my family. Nor does ovarian or uterine cancer. Colon cancer is about the extent of my history, on my dad's side. I knew there was some genetics involved in breast cancer, so for my six years of mammograms, I honestly just went through the motions, because I genuinely believed I was "exempt" from it because no one in my family had ever had it. No cousins, aunts, grandmas—no one. I had nothing to worry about. I was a very healthy and fit forty-five-year-old. Certainly, it was nothing. I made my appointment to have that annoying little fleck biopsied so I could scratch that off my list. The appointment was at the hospital where my OB's office was. The doctor agreed after the procedure and reviewing the films that I really had nothing to worry about; he felt certain it was benign. But the next day, on April 8, 2014, while enjoying my favorite salad at Taco Diner with one of my best friends, I got the dreaded phone call. "I'm sorry." That's really all I remember my doctor saying as the restaurant started spinning and the tears began to roll down my cheeks.
>
> —Char

From there, Char was referred to a surgeon. She made her appointment for a lumpectomy; the surgeon assured her the cells were tightly contained and a lumpectomy should do the trick. However, when the removed tissue was biopsied, there were "positive margins," meaning that they did not get all the cancer out.

So Char immediately made her appointment for another surgery with the same surgeon. He would "carve" a larger chunk of tissue out to have a better chance of getting it all out. That sounded fine with Char. But when his office called to confirm the appointment, something wasn't sitting right with her. She listened to her intuition. She met with two close friends, who insisted she get her game face on and take control of her situation. "Get off your ass and get a second opinion," they told her. "Now is not the time to sit back and take the easy route."

> I also called another dear friend, my friend Eileen who was living with stage IV metastatic breast cancer. Eileen's reaction surprised me—she was angry at me for not reaching out sooner, mad with the surgeon who had "already screwed up," and angry that I had the nerve even to consider going back to him. She brought to my attention that I still wasn't even able to say the word *cancer* and that I was still calling it "the C-word." She told me that if I were to remember nothing else from our conversation, I should remember that she was only angry and yelling at me because she loved me and needed to knock some sense into me. She settled down and gave me comforting "cancer for beginners" advice, starting with mentioning the National Cancer Institute and the Breast Cancer Research Foundation, and the next day I had a referral for a local surgical oncologist at

a new hospital. And three days after that I had
an appointment.

—Char

Char's new oncological surgeon spent several hours with her
reviewing her biopsy and lumpectomy results. She suggested to
Char that they "start over" with a more radical lumpectomy before
jumping to any conclusions. So in May, Char went in for surgery.
The surgeon was late starting Char's surgery because she insisted
that her pathologist review Char's biopsy results to double-check
the positive margins. Come to find out, the report from the previous hospital appeared to be inaccurate by the surgeon's standards,
but still, the surgeon felt it best to stick with the plan to remove a
more substantial chunk of breast tissue.

When my biopsy results came back, I was just
crushed. More positive margins. The biopsy
indicated that although I was stage 0 and non-
invasive, my cancer cells appeared to be more
widespread and "speckled" throughout my
right breast, like a shotgun pattern. There was
no guarantee that more surgery would remove
all of them, so I decided to go with a mastectomy—"And while you're at it, Doc, take them
both." My breasts had become my enemy.

—Char

Char decided to use her body tissue to rebuild both of her
breasts naturally instead of going with breast implants. To do this,
it required one very long surgery (ten hours) where they removed
"chunks" of tissue from her stomach and from under her butt and
built new breasts out of these four chunks. They reconnected the
blood flow in all six donor sites, and then they waited seventy-two

hours, with Char in ICU, to make sure that the blood was indeed flowing. Blood indeed flowed. Char was fortunate to have 100 percent survival of all four flaps.

> Recovery from that was awful! I thought I'd made a huge mistake because I couldn't functionally use my arms, legs, or core. I could only walk hunched over. I had six drains hanging from me, and I was "leaking" from every incision. What was I supposed to do, and how would I ever function at home? However, with each passing day, I got stronger and could straighten my limbs and core a little more. I quickly knew I would be okay and that I had made the right decision. Several revision surgeries later, here I am healthy and, for the most part, "normal"-looking again, minus the scars, which remind me daily of my triumphs.
>
> —Char

Char had what is called contralateral prophylactic mastectomy, or CPM, which is prophylactic surgery to remove a contralateral breast [the other breast, unaffected by cancer] during breast cancer surgery. CPM reduces the risk of breast cancer in that breast, although it is not yet known whether this risk reduction translates into longer survival for the patient. However, doctors often discourage contralateral prophylactic mastectomy for women with cancer in one breast who do not meet the criteria of being at very high risk of developing a contralateral breast cancer. For such women, the risk of developing another breast cancer, either in the same or the contralateral breast, is very small, especially if they receive adjuvant chemotherapy or hormone therapy as part of their cancer treatment.[1]

However, everyone has the right to make what they feel is the best decision for themselves. A recent study looked at reasons for individuals not in the high breast cancer risk category who still opted for CPM.

> Adeyiza Momoh, M.D., a reconstruction surgeon at the University of Michigan Comprehensive Cancer Center's Breast Cancer Center, and his colleagues published two studies in 2016 seeking to understand patients' decisions. Findings below were reasons women decided for CPM:
>
> A. The No. 1 concern was *worry about recurrence* when women made decisions for CPM, even though patients acknowledged being informed about the actual risks. And, again, those expressing the most anxiety were those who chose CPM with many believing that they faced significant risks despite being told otherwise by their doctors.
> B. Also, a *desire for breast symmetry* played a supporting role for patients choosing CPM. Even though CPM comes with higher complication rates and may not be an absolute medical necessity, this research shows that it may be the right choice for some patients, specifically for reasons of relief of worry.[2]

As for *BRCA1/BRCA2* mutation carriers who receive a diagnosis of breast cancer (in one breast) before age forty, studies have shown the risk of a contralateral breast cancer [breast cancer in the other

breast] reaches nearly 50 percent in the ensuing twenty-five years.
Contralateral breast cancer risk for *BRCA* carriers depends on age
at first breast cancer and on the affected *BRCA* gene.[3]

CHAPTER

—— 25 ——

Naked Lady Lilies

Synchronicity: A meaningful coincidence of two or
more events where something other than the
probability of chance is involved.[1]
—Carl Jung

Even though I have had my ovaries out and a prophylactic bilateral mastectomy, I am still monitored closely. Every six months I go to my high-risk oncologist, Dr. McKeen. At her office, I undergo manual breast exams; blood work, including CA-125 (ovarian marker) and CA-19-9 (pancreatic marker); and tumor marker tests, and every few years she orders me a bone density scan. Dr. McKeen doesn't mess around with *BRCA* and pays close attention to any changes to anything in my body. Because of the findings of additional history of cancer in my family, I had my second colonoscopy in January of 2016, as well as an EUS (endoscopic ultrasound, to check my pancreas) with a gastroenterologist. I go to a gastroenterologist who is knowledgeable about *BRCA* mutations.

It was March 7, 2016, and I was due for my six-month checkup. Everything was fine, or so I thought.

Robin, Dr. McKeen's nurse, started my manual breast exam. "I know I feel a lot of breasts, but I'm pretty sure I've never felt this before on you."

"What!?" I answered back abruptly, trying to comprehend what she was saying. *BRCA* anxiety was back.

Am I seriously going to be in the exceedingly small percentage of women who get breast cancer after a prophylactic bilateral double mastectomy? Is this the day I am going to get a cancer diagnosis, a breast cancer diagnosis?

I am vigilant, still continually feeling my breasts and under my armpits and pressing my chest area for any lump or bump. I had not felt anything. How was Robin feeling something?

"Right here around twelve o'clock at the top of your nipple, there is a palpable nodule," Robin continued.

The phrase *palpable nodule* brought more than a palpable lump to my throat. My advocate voice spoke up. "Can Dr. McKeen please come in and feel?"

"Sure," she said.

With her head remaining down looking at the chart, and after a quick hello, Dr. McKeen, wearing her white coat and not wasting a moment of her time, examined my reconstructed breasts. "Sometimes reconstructed breasts can be lumpy," she said as she manually pressed around my reconstructed breasts. "Let's get an ultrasound."

She booked me for a breast ultrasound the next day.

Xanax was back.

I decided I didn't want to tell anyone or worry them needlessly. I was so over myself and my medical issues, and sometimes I thought other people were tired of hearing about them too. This shit was unquestionably exhausting.

I didn't even tell Sista.

The morning of March 8, I turned on the eighties music station in the minivan to relax me. I was sure to know all the words
to whatever song was playing, and singing along at the top of my
lungs would get me out of my head.

My cell phone rang. I saw the number. It was Sista.

I didn't answer.

*I will call her later, when I know something. I definitely don't want
to worry her needlessly.*

My cell phone then chimed. Sista was now texting me.

Sista: I need to talk to you. Very important! Please call me.

I read Sista's text at a stoplight and thought, *Shit. Uh-oh. I'd better
call her back. Something might be up with Dad, as he has not been well.*
So I called her.

"Hi. Where are you?" Sista answered. "Are you going somewhere important?"

"Um, well," I said, "why?"

"Well, is it somewhere important?" Sista asked again.

I was debating what to say. *What do I tell her?*

"Um, why? What's up?" I asked straightforwardly, trying not to
clue her in to my anxiety or my appointment.

Sista paused for a second and then continued. "I was in the
shower this morning, and I found a lump."

No words came out of my mouth. I couldn't process what I was
hearing.

"Hello? You there?" Sista said, breaking a prolonged silence.

I didn't even know what to say to Sista, but somehow I managed
to get the following out: "Um, you just asked me if I was going
somewhere important. You are not going to believe this . . . I went
for my checkup with Dr. McKeen yesterday, and, uh, they found
a lump."

"*Whaaatt!*" Sista said, completely dumbfounded.

"I can't make this shit up," I shot back.

In unison, we both muttered, "OMG."

"Is it your left or right breast?" I asked.

"Right," Sista said.

"OMG," I said, "mine too."

I continued, "Where is it? Mine's at twelve o'clock at the top of my nipple."

"*Noooo!*" Sista responded, not believing what she was hearing. "Mine too!"

"OMG," I said.

"OMG," she said.

"WTF?" I said.

Both of us kept repeating "this is crazy" over and over again, thoroughly bowled over by what was happening.

We are three thousand miles apart—with a lump in the same breast, in the same spot, on the same day! How is this happening?

I arrived at my appointment and got my breast ultrasound. Sista and I continued to talk by text.

• • •

TEXTS BETWEEN ME AND SISTA

Tuesday, March 8, 2016

Me: All done. Radiologist not overly concerned. He didn't see anything, although he feels the lumpiness. He says reconstructed breasts are reconstructed and can be lumpy, etc. Although I have a feeling Dr. McKeen may still want me to have an MRI. Calling you now.

Me: Did you make it there?

Sista: Here at my breast surgeon's office. Had an ultrasound, and she is waiting to discuss results with the radiologist. She is taking it out today no matter what. She is not sure but thinks it could be a piece of dead fat from the fat grafting? Crazy. Will keep you posted.

Me: Okay. It is crazy.

Sista: Did the biopsy, but my doctor doesn't think it is anything to worry about. Since I lost weight, maybe just a piece of fat that had calcified and surfaced? She cut it out, and I have a small incision.

Me: Okay. You okay? Talk in a.m.?

Sista: Yes, fine. Flying back at 7:00 a.m. to SF.

• • •

Wednesday, March 9, 2016

Me: Hi. How u?

Sista: Okay. Back in SF at the office. Taking it easy today because I have a bandage on and it is a little bit sore. Will be okay, I hope. Go back for a follow-up next week.

Me: When is [the result of] your biopsy back?

Me: They want me to have [an] MRI.

Sista: Not sure. Hopefully this week, but she was not really concerned. She really thinks that it was some dead fat from the fat grafting. It did not feel like the tissue of a tumor. You thought they would make you do an MRI.

Me: Yes, my gut said they would. The radiologist was not really concerned with me either. But I think it is smart you had a biopsy, and I have an MRI. This way there is an absolute answer.

Me: Are you telling Mom, or no?

Sista: Yes, I will, because I have to be careful lifting and we are leaving for Scottsdale on Friday.

Me: Oh, okay.

Tuesday, March 15, 2016

Me: Hi, Sista. How are you? How was the trip? Did you hear back from your doctor? I'm not getting my MRI until we get back from vacation. Text me or call me. Love you!

Sista: My results are just fine. Going for a follow-up on Thursday. Have fun, and don't worry.

• • •

Monday, March 28, 2016

Me: Hi. MRI is done. All good. Phew! It was nothing! I told the radiologist about this happening to us at the same time, a lump, in the same breast, same spot.

Me: The radiologist's response: "Perhaps it was a sympathy lump for your sister."

• • •

CHAPTER

—— 26 ——

BRaCA Shmaka

Lillian, for so long I have felt you. You have given me signs. You have been there for me, your pull, your guidance, your warnings. I have felt your love. I have sensed your presence and heard your whispers. You have nudged me to share your story, our story, our family story. "Make my death mean something, Amy. Use your voice. Press forward, Amy. Share. It's the right thing to do." Unfortunately, ours is a story that so many other families share.

We may not have a traditional grandmother and granddaughter relationship, one where I can hop up on your lap, share lunch with you, or spend the afternoon playing cards or going shopping with you. However, our kinship and connection are undeniable. We are connected by DNA but also in heart and spirit.

While home on a recent visit, I did finally talk to Dad about you. I approached him where he was most comfortable, sitting on his already worn-out corner of the new den couch. I knew this wasn't going to be an easy conversation. Dad was apprehensive and sarcastic, agreeable yet irritated. Not that you would know who they are, Lillian, but Dad responded to me and sounded exactly like a real combination of Larry David and Archie Bunker. "So," he said abruptly, "you want to talk about that BRaCA shmaka?"

Dad speaks very easily about sports and business. He loves giving speeches and making seating charts, his left hand scribbling names and table numbers with a black felt pen in one of his large white notepads. He scribbles until he gets it just right, the way he wants it. Dad also feels free giving you his two cents on your life as he sees it. He is unapologetic giving you his unasked-for opinion. He will sit down with you and analyze company personnel for hours or give you a sermon on what you do right and what you do wrong. On the outside, he can be short-tempered and callous. On the inside, his family and everyone's health is more important to him than anything else, even baseball. He is humble and hugely philanthropic. Some of the traits that have served Dad well in business have caused strain in some of his relationships, the one between him and me included.

I want you to know that I have come to understand my dad, Lillian—my dad, your son. Dad is strong. He is a survivor and is who he is out of his reality and necessity. Losing you when he was seven years old could have been nothing but traumatic for him. You were here, and then you were gone. He lost what made him safe, what made him comforted. He lost his nurturer, part of his heart; he lost you, his mom.

While he doesn't typically have a hard time sharing his thoughts, I could tell it was tough for Dad to have this conversation. As I asked him questions about you, he was transported back to the shell of a young boy trying to make sense of it all. He doesn't remember much about you, Lillian. Dad spoke very slowly and very softly and barely got out one sentence. "I remember her being sick all the time, in bed, only feeling better when we were in Miami and in the warm weather."

He doesn't remember you taking him to school, cooking for him, baking, fixing him breakfast, helping him do homework, or even tucking him in at night. I tried to pull some memory out of him, but on his face remained a blank, empty stare. I soon realized his reality must be similar to that of other adults who lost a parent way too early, when both child and parent were way too young.

His profound sense of loss became astoundingly apparent in our conversation. Back then he was a young boy who just wanted your love, a mother's love. While he couldn't recall memories, I realized his sad eyes told me the whole story.

So, Lillian, I decided to share with Dad the title of *Resurrection Lily* and the many reasons why I chose it. I also told him that Sista and I feel you with us; we feel nudges and whispers from you and believe these have helped both of us to save our lives. I told Dad about the letter that I found about you in his office closet. Although I didn't fully understand what it meant at the time, I said to him that something must have spoken to me. I said that I went back to Florida insisting on a baseline mammogram in 2003 before I was thirty-five years old, even though recommendations back then were to start mammograms at age forty. I also shared with him a bit about Gilda Radner and told him that I read an article on ovarian cancer right before Sista had called me to tell me about her bloating and symptoms—and that I told her to get her butt to the doctor.

Dad listened to me share, and it was the first time in my life that I saw part of him look somewhat healed. His eyes and smile contained a joyful innocence that was recognizable to me as the same joyful innocence in the photo of you holding him when he was a little boy.

I asked Dad just one last question.

"So, Dad, what do you remember about your mom, about Lillian? Anything?"

"Well," he said, pausing, searching, scratching his head. He was thinking . . . and thinking.

He thought for a while.

I waited . . . and waited.

"Well," Dad finally said, again very softly and slowly but very calmly, "I do remember that she was a very kind, caring woman. And she would do something, well, because it was . . . the right thing to do."

As Dad said those last five words, the feeling flooded me; it was as if the most beautiful volcano had gently erupted, rapidly pouring sweet, warm lava through my veins, comforting me from head to toe.

There you are.

Those words. Exactly what I have felt from you, Lillian: nudging me forward to speak up and out, to save lives, to write this book.

Serendipity, synchronicity, coincidence, intuition, telepathy?

Genetics?

Love?

What I know for sure is that both your life and your death have allowed me to live, to love and be loved, and to remain breathing.

So every day and with every breath, I breathe you in . . .

I breathe you in.

Amy Byer Shainman
BRCA Responder
Providing education, advocacy and support surrounding *BRCA*
& other hereditary cancer syndromes.
Website: www.brcaresponder.com

Find Amy on Twitter, Facebook, Pinterest, Instagram, and LinkedIn.
@BRCAresponder

BRCA Responder's
BRCA/hereditary cancer book and movie list:
tinyurl.com/*BRCA*books

Pink & Blue: Colors of Hereditary Cancer is available on iTunes and
Google Play. The film continues to screen throughout the world and
is available for screenings in your area through Tugg—tugg.com

Website: pinkandbluemovie.com
Twitter: @pinkandbluedoc
Pink & Blue 2 is currently in production.

Acknowledgments

Thank you to everyone who said to me, "I think that it's great you are writing a book."

Sista. My rock, my Sista. I love you. The book is done!

First, a huge thank you to Ellen Matloff, MS, CGC. I am beyond grateful to you for your expert contributions throughout this book, your continued support, our #GenCSM partnership, and your friendship.

I could not have completed this project without your invaluable insights and contributions: Jan Byer; Dr. John Rimmer; Dr. David Lickstein; Dr. Elisabeth McKeen; Dr. Pamela Munster; Dr. Theodora Ross; Dr. Howard Goodman; Professor Timothy Rebbeck; Conni Murphy, ARNP, RNC; Georgia Hurst; Alan Blassberg; Eric Cecere; Patricia Hoke Simpson; Valerie Brock Jacobs; Tiffany Kenney Wiseman; Felicia Rodriguez; Julie Mak, MS, CGC; Craig Tracy; Debby Ganc; Jessica Tyson; LeRoy Rodgers; Karen Malkin-Lazarovitz; Charlotte Wilkerson Gajewski; Frank Bruno; Lisa M. Guzzardi, RN; Aimee Brown, MS, CGC; Meredith L. Seidel, MS, LCGC; Carol Love; Alix Troast; Lex Rofeberg; Alexandria Farris; Bonnie Dillion; Alisa Jeras, RN; Danielle Bonadies; Gwen Ash; Archway Publishing Group; Kirstin Andrews, Brooke Warner; Jessica Vogel; Jon Shainman.

A special note of appreciation to: Dr. Rimmer, thank you for your compassion, expertise, infinite patience, bedside manner, and continued support. Dr. Lickstein, thank you for your genuine care and aesthetic extraordinaire. Dr. Elisabeth McKeen, thank you for those first appointments and the continued care.

A special shout-out to health care providers: Dr. Jeffrey Litt; Dr. Marc Kaufmann; Dr. Donna Pinelli; Dr. Linda Pao; Dr. Eliot Ellis; Dr. Elise Chang Hillman; Dr. Gloria Hakkarainen; Cathy Marinak, ARNP; Deidra Brown-Brinson, ARNP; Robin Stevens, ARNP.

Wendy Chin Thompson, only you would drop everything to be with me before my mastectomy. Thank you for calming and centering me as you always do, *my forever friend*. I love you!

Charlotte Wilkerson Gajewski, thank you for being there for me after my mastectomy and making me feel warm, cozy, and sore from so much laughing! Thank you for not hesitating to share your personal story publicly when I asked and thank you in advance for all future Rice Krispies Treats. I love you, my *BFF!*

Allysa Friedman and Amy Labell, I am beyond appreciative of all your pre- and postsurgery in-person support, meal train, play-dates, gatherings, and continued friendship.

Joseph Sedillo and Megan Juscen Leveille, thank you for your fierce and loyal friendship and most excellent care of Sista. Diane Shader Smith, thank for your wisdom, support, friendship, and continued guidance. Michele Lackovic and Teri Smieja, you were my cheerleaders early on in this project. Thank you both for that love and motivation.

Love and thanks to the entire *Pink & Blue: Colors of Hereditary Cancer* cast and crew.

Alan Blassberg, my brother from another mother; Sammy; Sista—serendipity, Sal.

Love to Stephanie Swarz, Mario, Bodhi and Maya, and Ellie.

To all the patient advocates, a huge thank you for doing what you do on a daily basis. You inspire me to continue my advocacy efforts.

Friends and family, near and far, thank you all for your friendship, continued support, and love.

Special recognition to: Dyann Yarish Gormezano, MD; Lori Goldman Reddy; Rochelle Batt Kushner; Julie Mitchell; Christine Steel; Sarah Kivel; Leslie Osborne; Paul Osborne; Genevieve Stroud; Shelly Wisner Machell; Jennifer Shakerdge; Nancy Berman; Margot Matot; Georgia Hurst; Frank Bruno; Ilene Smiley; Valerie Staggs; Roberta Meshel; Patti and Richard Newcomb; Gali and Rabbi Alon Levkovitz; Dawn Williams; Marilyn "Nantie" Drake; Shelley Dickinson; Ellen Booth Church and Jerry Levine; Marla and Barry Shainman; my brothers and their families.

Special love and appreciation to you, Mom and Dad Byer.

I love you, Jon, Brooke, and Ben, more than anything.

Hereditary Breast and Ovarian Cancer Syndrome

Who Should Consider Genetic Counseling and Testing?
Guidelines Have Expanded.

Approximately 10% of all cancer is thought to be hereditary.

At least 15% of ovarian cancer is suspected to be hereditary.

RISK FACTORS

History of one of the following at any age:

- ovarian cancer
- pancreatic cancer
- metastatic prostate cancer
- male breast cancer

Individual with breast cancer and the following:

- diagnosis of breast cancer is before age 50
- breast cancer is triple negative and before age 60
- multiple primary breast cancers in individual

Individual with breast cancer and family history of:

- breast cancer before age 50
- invasive ovarian cancer
- male breast cancer
- pancreatic cancer
- high grade/metastatic prostate cancer
- more than two relatives with histories of breast cancer

Other risk factors:

- Jewish ancestry and breast cancer or high grade prostate cancer (Gleason score > 7)
- Multiple BRCA-related cancers in one person (e.g. someone with two breast primaries, with both breast and ovarian, or with breast and pancreatic cancers)
- Known pathogenic genetic variant (mutation) in the family (e.g. pathogenic BRCA1/2 mutation)
- A pathogenic BRCA1/2 variant found on genetic testing of a tumor sample (somatic variant)

If someone does not meet the above criteria for genetic counseling themselves but a close relative does, genetic counseling may still be indicated. A genetic counselor can determine whether genetic testing is appropriate and who in the family should be tested first.

MY GENE COUNSEL | www.mygenecounsel.com | info@mygenecounsel.com

Based on guidelines from the National Comprehensive Cancer Network (NCCN), which is a consortium of cancer centers with experts in the management of hereditary cancer. The NCCN updates their guidelines for risk management for people with hereditary risk for cancer, based on the latest research. In general, NCCN guidelines dictate the standard of care for high-risk patients in the United States.

How Much Does a *BRCA* Gene Mutation Increase Cancer Risk?

Cancer risk percentages in *BRCA* carriers vary slightly depending on the resource. Statistics may change depending on the new research. Below are the most recent statistics on cancer risk in *BRCA* carriers from the Basser Center for *BRCA*.

The cancers most commonly associated with *BRCA* mutations are breast (male and female), ovarian, prostate, and pancreatic cancers, as well as melanoma.

Lifetime *BRCA1* and *BRCA2* Cancer Risks

TYPE OF CANCER	WOMEN			MAN		
	Woman with a BRCA1 mutation	Woman with a BRCA2 mutation	Average woman in US without mutation	Man with a BRCA1 mutation	Man with a BRCA2 mutation	Average man in US without mutation
Breast	60-75%	50-70%	13%	1-5%	5-10%	0.1%
Ovarian	30-50%	10-20%	1-2%	-	-	-
Prostate	-		-	*†	15-25%*	16%
Pancreatic	2-3%	3-5%	1%	2-3%	3-5%	1%
Melanoma	-	3-5%	1-2%	-	3-5%	1-2%
Uterine	*†	-	2-3%	-	-	-

† There may be a very small increased risk of uterine cancer in BRCA1 carriers, particularly those who have taken tamoxifen. More research is needed before this association is fully understood.

† Although there is no convincing evidence of overall increased risk of prostate cancer, men with BRCA1 mutations may develop prostate cancer at a younger age than men in the general population. BRCA2 mutations are associated with an increased risk of prostate cancer, which also can be of earlier onset.

—No known increased cancer risk

The Basser Center for *BRCA* at Penn Medicine's Abramson Cancer Center is the first comprehensive center for the research, treatment, and prevention of *BRCA*-related cancers. Devoted to advancing care for people affected by *BRCA* gene mutations, the Basser Center's unique model provides funding for collaborative research, education, and outreach programs around the world.

What Are the Screening and Management Guidelines for *BRCA1* and *BRCA2* Carriers?

WOMEN

- Breast MRI (magnetic resonance imaging) annually for people between the ages of twenty-five and twenty-nine (breast MRI is preferred because of the theoretical risk of radiation exposure in mutation carriers)
- Breast MRI and mammogram for people thirty to seventy-four years old
- Individualized based on family history if breast cancer diagnosis before age thirty is present
- Consider transvaginal ultrasound and CA-125 blood test every six to twelve months

RISK REDUCTION FOR WOMEN

- *BRCA1*: RRSO (risk-reducing salpingo-oophorectomy) between the ages of thirty-five and forty
- *BRCA2*: RRSO between the ages of forty and forty-five
- Discuss mastectomy

MEN

- Breast self-exam at thirty-five years of age
- Clinical breast exam every twelve months starting at thirty-five years of age
- Prostate cancer screening at forty-five years of age

WOMEN AND MEN

- Individualized pancreatic cancer and melanoma screenings based on cancers observed in the family. Full body skin exam and melanoma eye exam. EUS (endoscopic ultrasound) and MRI are considered the most accurate tools for pancreatic imaging and do not involve ionizing radiation.

Derived from NCCN Guidelines, Genetic/Familial High-Risk Assessment Breast and Ovarian, January 2018. The National Comprehensive Cancer Network (NCCN) is a consortium of cancer centers with experts in management of hereditary cancer. The NCCN updates their guidelines for risk management for people with hereditary risk for cancer, based on the latest research. In general, NCCN guidelines dictate the standard of care for high-risk patients in the United States. Visit them at nccn.org.

Find a Certified Genetic Counselor

To find a certified genetic counselor near you or to speak to one by telephone, please go to the National Society of Genetic Counselors at www.nsgc.org, or call them at (312) 321-6834.

To ensure you make the best health care decisions for yourself, understand current health screening guidelines, and understand genetic testing guidelines, please speak with a certified genetic counselor before and after any genetic testing.

Physicians, learn how to incorporate genetic counseling into your practice:
https://www.nsgc.org/page/incorporate-genetic-counseling

Hereditary Cancer Programs

Hereditary cancer programs provide care for people affected by *BRCA* mutations.
The following centers are the ones mentioned in this book:

UCSF Center for *BRCA* Research – http://brca.ucsf.edu/
To make an appointment with the Hereditary Cancer Clinic, please call (415) 353-9797.

Basser Center for *BRCA* – basser.org
To schedule an appointment at Penn Medicine for genetic risk evaluation or management of hereditary cancer, please contact the Cancer Risk Evaluation Program at (215) 349-9093.

University of Texas Southwestern Medical Center
http://www.utswmedicine.org/cancer/programs/cancer-genetics/
To schedule an appointment with a cancer genetics specialist, call (214) 645-8300.

Cancer Genetics Program at Good Samaritan Medical Center
https://www.goodsamaritanmc.com/our-services/cancer/genetic-screening
Call for an appointment: (561) 650-6084.

BRCA Cancer Risks

As mentioned in the advocacy sections, *BRCA* cancer risk percentages vary slightly depending on the resource. Following are *BRCA* cancer risk percentages from two additional resources:

UCSF CENTER FOR *BRCA* RESEARCH

The purpose of the UCSF Center for *BRCA* Research is to provide a central resource for families with *BRCA* and other mutations to receive personalized care and planning for their long-term health and well-being.

Breast Cancer
Lifetime risk in general population of women: 12 percent
Lifetime risk for *BRCA1-positive* or *BRCA2*-positive women: 50–85 percent
Risk for women with a *BRCA1* or *BRCA2* mutation who have had breast cancer of developing second breast cancer in either the same or the opposite breast: 40–60 percent

Breast Cancer in Men
Lifetime risk in the general population (men): 0.1 percent
Lifetime risk for men with *BRCA1* or *BRCA2*: 5–10 percent

Ovarian Cancer

Lifetime risk of ovarian in the general population: 1–2 percent
Lifetime risk of ovarian cancer for a woman with *BRCA1* mutation: 40 percent
Lifetime risk of ovarian cancer for a woman with *BRCA2* mutation: 20 percent

THE NATIONAL CANCER INSTITUTE

The National Cancer Institute (NCI) is the US federal government's principal agency for cancer research and training. NCI leads, conducts, and supports cancer research across the nation to advance scientific knowledge and help all people live longer, healthier lives.

Breast Cancer

Lifetime risk in general population of women: about 12 percent
Lifetime risk for *BRCA1*-positive women: 55–65 percent by age seventy
Lifetime risk for *BRCA2*-positive women: 45 percent by age seventy

Ovarian Cancer

Lifetime risk for general population: about 1.3 percent
Lifetime risk of woman with *BRCA1* mutation: 39 percent by age seventy
Lifetime risk of woman with *BRCA2*: 11–17 percent by age seventy

Reader Discussion Guide

- Discuss the title *Resurrection Lily* and its theme throughout the book.

- Was there anything you specifically related to in the author's story?

- What did you learn that you didn't know before?

- Without using any names (for privacy), do you know someone who has taken a genetic test and made similar or very different decisions based on his or her genetic test results? How has this book helped you understand genetic testing and genetic counseling?

- Discuss the "Angelina Jolie effect." What do you remember about the news coverage surrounding Angelina's op-ed articles in *The New York Times*? How has the author's story changed your opinion of Jolie (if it has at all)?

- How has the author's story changed or not changed your opinion of prophylactic surgery?

- Discuss how different cultures and ethnic groups may handle communication surrounding cancer risk? How may an individual's religious views guide decisions about their health?

Genetic Counseling Student Discussion Guide

- Every patient has different experiences that factor into cancer risk-management decision-making. Compare and contrast how the author's cancer risk-management decisions (finding out she carries a *BRCA1* mutation at age forty) may differ from a woman finding out she carries a *BRCA1* mutation at age twenty-five. In the clinical setting, how would you counsel these two women differently? Discuss for both *BRCA1* and *BRCA2*.

- Discuss how genetic counseling for a male may differ at different ages. Discuss for both Hereditary Breast and Ovarian Cancer syndrome and Lynch syndrome.

- Discuss cultural factors that may influence genetic counseling, genetic testing, and cancer risk-management decision-making. Discuss for both females and males in various cultures.

- How would you counsel a patient who has had misinterpreted genetic testing results?

- What are ways that you can advocate for patients or encourage patients to advocate for themselves?

- Discuss your level of confidence and also knowing your limitations as a genetic counselor. Discuss why, with the constantly evolving science, sometimes "I don't know" is the right answer.

- Discuss listening to patients and their individual concerns. How can you use your counseling time wisely to address your patient's specific concerns thoroughly and not get trapped into focusing on your own agenda?

- What are ways you can go the extra mile for patients?

Sources

PREFACE

[1] "Genetic Counseling and Testing." n.d. Basser.org. https://www.basser.org/patients-families/genetic-counseling-and-testing.

[2] "Resurrection Lily." n.d. Gardeningcentral.org. http://www.gardening central.org/resurrection_lily/resurrection_lily.html.

OTHER SOURCES

Armstrong, Katrina, Janet Weiner, Barbara Weber, and David Asch. 2003. "Early Adoption of BRCA1/2 Testing: Who and Why." Genetics in Medicine. https://www.nature.com/articles/gim200320.

"BRCA1 and BRCA2 Gene Mutations." Know: BRCA. Accessed May 11, 2018. https://www.knowbrca.org/Learn/BRCA1-and-BRCA2 gene mutations.

Friedman, Sue. 2018. "PARP Inhibitors and Hereditary Cancer: What's New?" Facing Our Risk Of Cancer Empowered. http://www.facingourrisk.org/get-involved/HBOC-community/BRCA-HBOC-blogs/FORCE/parp-inhibitor-research/parp-inhibitors-and-hereditary-cancer-whats-new/.

"NCI Dictionary of Cancer Terms." 2018. National Cancer Institute. https://www.cancer.gov/publications/dictionaries/cancer-terms/def/parp-inhibitor.

Vogue, Ariane. 2013. "Supreme Court Rejects Gene Patent." ABC News. http://abcnews.go.com/Politics/supreme-court-strikes-brca-gene-patent/story?id=19392299.

PART I. SOIL, SEEDS, AND LEAVES

CHAPTER 1: RESURRECTION LILY

[1] "History of ACS Recommendations for the Early Detection of Cancer in People without Symptoms." n.d. Cancer.org. http://www.cancer.org/healthy/findcancerearly/cancerscreeningguidelines/chronological-history-of-acs-recommendations.

CHAPTER 2: ROOT FEELING

[1] Powell, Diane Hennacy. 2010. *The ESP Enigma: The Scientific Case for Psychic Phenomena*. New York: Walker.

[2] Radford, Benjamin. 2018. "The Riddle of Twin Telepathy." Live Science. https://www.livescience.com/45405-twin-telepathy.html.

[3] Prindle Fierro, Pamela. 2018. "Twin Telepathy: Separating Fact From Fiction." Verywell Family. https://www.verywellfamily.com/twin-telepathy-2447130.

OTHER SOURCES

Ambury, James M. "Socrates (469–399 B.C.E.)" The Internet Encyclopedia of Philosophy. Accessed August 8, 2018. ISSN 2161-0002, https://www.iep.utm.edu/socrates/#SSH2bi.

Ray, Rachel. Review of *The ESP Enigma: The Scientific Case for Psychic Phenomena* by Diane Hennacy Powell. March 15, 2010. http://www.telegraph.co.uk/culture/books/bookreviews/7448932/The-ESP-Enigma-The-Scientific-Case-for-Psychic-Phenomena-by-Diane-Hennacy-Powell-review.html.

Stephens, Jessie. 2016. "Twin 'Telepathy' Definitely Exists, but Not for the Reason You Might Think." Mamamia. https://www.mamamia.com.au/do-twins-have-esp-or-telepathy/.

Stephey, M.J. 2008. "The Science behind Psychic Phenomena." TIME.com. http://content.time.com/time/health/article/0,8599,1868287,00.html.

CHAPTER 3: BLOSSOM

Ebert, Roger. 1983. "Flashdance Movie Review & Film Summary (1983)." Rogerebert.com. https://www.rogerebert.com/reviews/flashdance-1983.

PART II. LILIES

CHAPTER 4: GILDA AND NORENE

[1] Norman, Abby. 2016. "Gene Wilder Was Right: Gilda Radner Didn't Have to Die, and We Need to Talk About Why She Did." Medium. https://medium.com/@abbymnorman/gene-wilder-was-right-gilda-radner-didnt-have-to-die-and-we-need-to-talk-about-why-she-did-b2797e01db28.

[2] Wilder, Gene. 1991. "Why Did Gilda Die?" PEOPLE.com. http://people.com/archive/cover-story-why-did-gilda-die-vol-35-no-21/.

[3] Wilder, Gene. 2016. "Gene Wilder's Tearful Goodbye to Wife Gilda Radner." PEOPLE.com. https://people.com/movies/gene-wilders-tearful-goodbye-to-wife-gilda-radner/

OTHER SOURCES

Karras, Steve. 2013. "Gilda Radner Remembered." Huffpost. https://www.huffingtonpost.com/steve-karras/gilda-radner-club_b_2366303.html.

Mower, Joan. 1991. "Gene Wilder Urges More Spending on Ovarian Cancer." Apnewsarchive.com. http://www.apnewsarchive.com/1991/Gene-

Wilder-Urges-More-Spending-on-Ovarian-Cancer/id-ad97408a5bbaa
14a75e44fdaee9cad5a.

CHAPTER 5: SISTA

[1] King, Carole. "I Feel the Earth Move." 1971. Colgems-EMI Music. Reprinted by permission of Hal Leonard LLC.

OTHER SOURCES

Wilder, Gene. 1991. "Why Did Gilda Die?" PEOPLE.com. http://people.com/archive/cover-story-why-did-gilda-die-vol-35-no-21/.

CHAPTER 6: KRISTIN

[1] Hearst Television Inc. on behalf of WPBF-TV. 2008. *A Personal Story: Kristin Hoke.* Video. https://www.youtube.com/watch?v=U4L1nF83IpA.

EMAILS BETWEEN ME, JON AND KRISTIN

"Ovarian, Fallopian Tube, & Primary Peritoneal Cancer Prevention." n.d. National Cancer Institute. https://www.cancer.gov/types/ovarian/hp/ovarian-prevention-pdq.

PART III. SUNLIGHT AND SHADE

CHAPTER 7: HAIL MARY

[1] "Penn's Basser Research Center For BRCA Names BRCA1 Founder Mary-Claire King Winner of the 2014 Basser Global Prize." 2014. Pennmedicine.org. https://www.pennmedicine.org/news/news-releases/2014/august/penns-basser-research-center-f.; "Mary-Claire King." Encyclopedia of World Biography. Encyclopedia.com. Accessed August 4, 2018. http://www.encyclopedia.com/history/encyclopedias-almanacs-transcripts-and-maps/mary-claire-king

[2] "Endometrial Cancer Treatment." n.d. National Cancer Institute. https://www. cancer.gov/types/uterine/patient/endometrial-treatment-pdq#section/_111.

[3] "Ovarian Cancer - Symptoms and Causes." n.d. Mayo Clinic. https://www. mayoclinic.org/diseases-conditions/ovarian-cancer/basics/definition/ con-20028096.; "Ovarian Cancer - Symptoms and Causes." n.d. Mayo Clinic. https://www. mayoclinic.org/diseases-conditions/ovarian-cancer/ symptoms-causes/ syc-20375941?p=1.

OTHER SOURCES

"How Am I Diagnosed?" n.d. Ovarian.org. http://ovarian.org/about-ovarian-cancer/how-am-i-diagnosed.

CHAPTER 8: ME

[1] "Who We Are Your MGC Founders." n.d. My Gene Counsel. https://www. mygenecounsel.com/leadership/.

[2] Mukherjee, Siddhartha. 2016. The Gene: An Intimate History. New York: Scribner.

CHAPTER 9: DR. MCKEEN

Steenhuysen, Julie. 2017. "Pregnancy after Breast Cancer Doesn't Raise Recurrence Risk – Study." U.S. https://www.reuters.com/article/us-health-cancer-fertility/pregnancy-after-breast-cancer-doesnt-raise-recurrence-risk-study-idUSKBN18U0GR.

JOURNAL ENTRIES AND EMAILS, JANUARY– JUNE 2010

Angelou, Maya. 2012. "Maya Angelou." Facebook.com. https://www.face book.com/MayaAngelou/posts/10151140563519796.

PART IV. PERENNIAL PATIENT

CHAPTER 10: DR. RIMMER

[1] White House Television (WHTV), "Maya Angelou's Poem 'On the Pulse of Morning.'" Clinton Digital Library. Accessed July 10, 2018. https://clinton. presidentiallibraries.us/items/show/15928.

OTHER SOURCES

"Triple Negative Breast Cancer Foundation®." n.d. Triple Negative Breast Cancer Foundation. https://tnbcfoundation.org/.

CHAPTER 11: FAT, TISSUE, WOMAN, ROAR

[1] "Vestibular Schwannoma (Acoustic Neuroma) and Neurofibromatosis." n.d. NIDCD. https://www.nidcd.nih.gov/health/vestibular-schwannoma -acoustic-neuroma-and-neurofibromatosis#ref4.

[2] "Density Facts." n.d. Areyoudenseadvocacy.org. http://areyoudenseadvocacy .org/facts.

OTHER SOURCES

Cappello, N. 2018. "Are You Dense: Nancy's Story." Areyoudense.org. Accessed July 10, 2018. https://www.areyoudense.org/stories/nancy/.

Dupree, Beth. 2013. "Living in Your 'GENES.'" The Buzz. https://drbethdupree .wordpress.com/2013/05/16/living-in-your-genes/.

Greenwood, Michael. 2013. "Study Launched to Find the Origins of Acoustic Neuromas." Medicine.Yale.edu. https://medicine.yale.edu/emergencymed/ news/article.aspx?id=5909.

"Metastatic Cancer." n.d. National Cancer Institute. https://www.cancer. gov/types/metastatic-cancer#what.

"The Yale University Acoustic Neuroma Study." n.d. Anausa.org. https:// www.anausa.org/resources/research/an-research/yale-university.

Thomas, Jamescia. 2012. "Tough Choices in Fight against Breast Cancer Gene." CNN. https://www.cnn.com/2012/10/26/health/brca-gene-ireporters/index. html.

PART V. REFLECTION POND

CHAPTER 12: LESSONS OF SELF-WORTH

[1] "How Am I Diagnosed?" n.d. Ovarian.org. http://ovarian.org/about-ovarian -cancer/how-am-i-diagnosed.

OTHER SOURCES

PDQ® Screening and Prevention Editorial Board. PDQ Ovarian, Fallopian Tube, and Primary Peritoneal Cancer Screening. Bethesda, MD: National Cancer Institute. Accessed August 3, 2018. https://www.cancer.gov/types/ ovarian/hp/ovarian screening pdq. [PMID: 26389336]

CHAPTER 13: LETTERS AND LILLIAN

Combs, Linda C. and Joseph B. Zwischenberger. "Fred W. Rankin, MD: A Man of Medicine during a Time of War and Change." *Journal of the American College of Surgeons* 212 4 (2011): e13–23.

Reply letter dated July 21, 1934, to Bo Byer from Fred W. Rankin, MD, used by permission of Doug Rankin, Fred Rankin's grandson.

PART VI. HONEY AND HORNETS

CHAPTER 14: SAVING A LIFE

[1] "Pikuach Nefesh". n.d. Jewishvirtuallibrary.org. https://www.jewishvirtual library.org/pikuach-nefesh.

[2] "Chai, Its Meaning and Signicance." n.d. Shiva.com. https://www.shiva. com/learning-center/commemorate/chai/.

OTHER SOURCES

Antoniou, A., P. D. Pharoah, S. Narod, et al. "Average Risks of Breast and Ovarian Cancer Associated with *BRCA1* or *BRCA2* Mutations Detected in Case Series Unselected for Family History: A Combined Analysis of 22 Studies." *American Journal of Human Genetics* 72, no. 5 (2003): 1117–30.

Basser Center for *BRCA*. n.d. Lifetime *BRCA1* And *BRCA2* Cancer Risks. Image. https://www.basser.org/patients-families/managing-cancer-risk.

"*BRCA* Mutations: Cancer Risk & Genetic Testing." n.d. National Cancer Institute. https://www.cancer.gov/about-cancer/causes-prevention/genetics/brca -fact-sheet#q2 and http://brca.ucsf.edu/breast-and-ovarian-cancer.

"Breast And Ovarian Cancer | Center For *BRCA* Research". 2018. Brca.Ucsf. Edu. https://brca.ucsf.edu/breast-and-ovarian-cancer.

Chen, S., and G. Parmigiani. 2007. "Meta-Analysis of *BRCA1* and *BRCA2* Penetrance." *Journal of Clinical Oncology* 25, no. 11: 1329–33.

Howlader, N., A. M. Noone, M. Krapcho, et al., eds. Posted to the SEER website April 2014. "SEER Cancer Statistics Review, 1975–2011." Based on November 2013 SEER data submission. http://seer.cancer.gov/csr/1975_2011/.

CHAPTER 15: PROPHYLACTIC SURGERIES, DRASTIC REACTIONS

[1] Klitzman R, Chung W. 2010. "The Process of Deciding about Prophylactic Surgery for Breast and Ovarian Cancer: Patient Questions, Uncertainties, and Communication." *American Journal of Medical Genetics* Part A. 152A:52–66. doi: 10.1002/ajmg.a.33068.; Dean, M. & E. A. Rauscher. 2017. "'It was an Emotional Baby': Previvors' Family Planning Decision-Making Styles about Hereditary Breast and Ovarian Cancer Risk." Journal of Genetic Counseling 26: 1301. https://doi.org/10.1007/s10897-017-0069-8; Collier, Roger. 2012. "Young Women with Breast Cancer Genes Face Tough Choices, Eighth of a Multipart Series on Genetic Testing." Ebook. CMAJ. http://www.cmaj.ca/content/cmaj/184/8/E401.full.pdf.

PART VII. HAMPERED HEALING GARDEN

CHAPTER 17: MORE TO SORT

[1] "Understanding Genetics: A New England Guide for Patients and Health Professionals." February 17, 2010. Washington DC: Genetic Alliance. https://www.ncbi.nlm.nih.gov/books/NBK132180/

CHAPTER 18: SOAKING THIS IN

[1] "*BRCA* Mutations: Cancer Risk & Genetic Testing." n.d. National Cancer Institute. https://www.cancer.gov/about-cancer/causes-prevention/genetics/brca-fact-sheet#q4.

CHAPTER 19: HEAVY LOAD

[1] Domchek, S. L., and A. M. Kaunitz. 2016. "Use of Systemic Hormone Therapy in *BRCA* Mutation Carriers." Ncbi.Nlm.Nih.gov. https://www.ncbi.nlm.nih.gov/pubmed/27504919.

OTHER SOURCES

Basser Center for *BRCA*. n.d. Lifetime *BRCA1* And *BRCA2 Cancer Risks*. Image. https://www.basser.org/patients-families/managing-cancer-risk.

Canto, M. I., F. Harinck, R. H. Hruban, et al. "International Cancer of the Pancreas Screening (CAPS): Consortium Summit on the Management of Patients with Increased Risk for Familial Pancreatic Cancer." Gut 62 (2013): 339–47.

Collier, Roger. 2012. *Young Women with Breast Cancer Genes Face Tough Choices, Eighth of a Multipart Series on Genetic Testing*. Ebook. CMAJ. http://www.cmaj. ca/content/cmaj/184/8/E401.full.pdf.

Colliver, Victoria. 2014. "For Cancer Specialists, Disease Can Make Them Better Doctors." Sfgate. http://www.sfgate.com/health/article/For-cancer-specialists-disease-can-make-them-5543259.php.

Domchek, Susan, and Andrew M. Kaunitz. 2016. "Use of Systemic Hormone Therapy In *BRCA* Mutation Carriers." *Menopause 23* (9): 1026-1027. doi:10.1097/ gme.0000000000000724.

Dunn, Lauren. 2016. "Doctor Targets Gene Mutations for Cancer Care." NBC News. https://www.nbcnews.com/health/cancer/doctor-targets-gene-mutations-cancer-care-n587486.

Groves, Alexandria, and Lisa Rezende, PhD. 2017. "Update on Hormone Therapy for Previvors." Facing Our Risk of Cancer Empowered. http://www. facingourrisk.org/get-involved/HBOC-community/BRCA-HBOC-blogs/ FORCE/menopause/update-hormone-therapy-previvors/.

"How Much Does a *BRCA* Gene Mutation Increase Cancer Risk?" Used by permission of Basser Center for *BRCA*.

National Public Radio. 2016. "Bad Luck or Bad Genes? Dealing with *BRCA* and 'A Cancer in the Family." Podcast. Fresh Air. https://www.npr.

org/2016/03/14/470371943/bad-luck-or-bad-genes-dealing-with-brca-and-a-cancer-in-the-family.

NCCN Clinical Practice Guidelines in Oncology (NCCN Guidelines®) Genetic/ Familial High-Risk Assessment: Breast and Ovarian. 2018. Ebook. Fort Washington: NCCN. https://www.nccn.org/professionals/physician_gls/pdf/genetics_screening.pdf.

"What Are the Screening and Management Guidelines for *BRCA1* and *BRCA2* Carriers?" Derived from NCCN Guidelines Genetic/Familial High-Risk Assessment Breast and Ovarian. Accessed August, 2018. (The National Comprehensive Cancer Network (NCCN) is a consortium of cancer centers with experts in the management of hereditary cancer. The NCCN updates its guidelines for risk management for people with hereditary risk for cancer, based on the latest research. In general, NCCN guidelines dictate the standard of care for high risk patients.) [In the United States]

"What Happens After Prophylactic Ovary Removal." 2012. Breastcancer. org. https://www.breastcancer.org/treatment/surgery/prophylactic_ovary/what_to_expect/after.

"What Is a Previvor?" Winter 2009. Newsletter. Facingourrisk.org. http://www.facingourrisk.org/understanding-brca-and-hboc/publications/newsletter/archives/2009winter/what-is-previvor.php.

PART VIII. REPURPOSED FLOWERS

CHAPTER 20: ANGELINA

[1] Jolie, Angelina. 2018. "Opinion | My Medical Choice by Angelina Jolie." Nytimes.com. http://www.nytimes.com/2013/05/14/opinion/my-medical-choice.html.

[2] Igoe, Katherine. 2016. "The 'Angelina Jolie' Effect." Hms.Harvard.edu. https://hms.harvard.edu/news/angelina-jolie-effect.; Kluger, Jeffrey. 2013. "The Angelina Effect: TIME'S New Cover Image Revealed." TIME.com.

http://healthland.time.com/2013/05/15/the-angelina-effect-times-new-cover-image-revealed/.

[3] Jolie Pitt, Angelina. 2018. "Opinion | Angelina Jolie Pitt: Diary of a Surgery." Nytimes.com. https://www.nytimes.com/2015/03/24/opinion/angelina-jolie-pitt-diary-of-a-surgery.html.

[4] "What Should I Know About Screening?" Centers for Disease Control and Prevention. Accessed August 1, 2018.; "Ovarian Cancer Screening." 2018. Moffitt Cancer Center. Accessed August 1, 2018. https://moffitt.org/cancers/ovarian-cancer/screening/.

OTHER SOURCES

"Cowden syndrome." 2018. [online] Genetics Home Reference. https://ghr.nlm.nih.gov/condition/cowden-syndrome#genes.

"Li-Fraumeni syndrome." 2018. [online] Genetics Home Reference. https://ghr.nlm.nih.gov/condition/li-fraumeni-syndrome#genes.

"Lynch syndrome." 2018. [online] Genetics Home Reference. https://ghr.nlm.nih.gov/condition/lynch-syndrome#genes.

Tucker, Karen Iris. 2014. "How Angelina Jolie Changed Things For People With BRCA Mutations." The Forward. https://forward.com/culture/204221/how-angelina-jolie-changed-things-for-people-with/.

PART IX. GARDENERS

CHAPTER 22: DOCTOR, DOCTOR

[1] Norman, Abby. 2016. "Gene Wilder Was Right: Gilda Radner Didn't Have to Die, and We Need to Talk About Why She Did." The Independent. http://www.independent.co.uk/voices/gene-wilder-death-gilda-radner-cancer-awareness-comedy-relationship-we-need-to-talk-about-it-a7217966.html.

[2] Wilder, Gene. 2016. "Gene Wilder's Tearful Goodbye to Wife Gilda Radner" PEOPLE.com. https://people.com/movies/gene-wilders-tearful-goodbye-to-wife-gilda-radner/.

[3] Wilder, Gene. 1991. "Why Did Gilda Die?" PEOPLE.com. http://people.com/archive/cover-story-why-did-gilda-die-vol-35-no-21/.

OTHER SOURCES

"Gilda Radner." n.d. Women Wiki. http://women.wikia.com/wiki/Gilda_Radner.

McIntosh, Whitney. 2016. "After Gilda Radner's Death, Gene Wilder Wrote a Heartbreaking Essay about Her Cancer Battle." Yahoo.com. https://www.yahoo.com/entertainment/gilda-radners-death-gene-wilder-042506298.html.

CHAPTER 23: GENETIC COUNSELING AND GENETIC TESTING

[1] "NSGC > Genetic Testing > Genetic Counseling vs. Genetic Testing." n.d. Aboutgeneticcounselors.com. http://aboutgeneticcounselors.com/Genetic-Testing/Genetic-Counseling-vs-Genetic-Testing.

[2] American Journal of Preventive Medicine (December 11, 2017): ii: S0749-3797(17)30638-4. https://doi.org/10.1016/j.amepre.2017.10.015. https://www.ncbi.nlm.nih.gov/m/pubmed/29241717/?i=5&from=brca#fft.

[3] "NSGC > Genetic Testing > Genetic Counseling vs. Genetic Testing." n.d. Aboutgeneticcounselors.com. http://aboutgeneticcounselors.com/Genetic-Testing/Genetic-Counseling-vs-Genetic-Testing.

[4] Inherited Cancer Registry July 2013 Newsletter/BRCA Testing: Supreme Court Update. 2013. Ebook. Tampa: Moffitt/ICARE. https://inheritedcancer.net/wp-content/uploads/2014/03/ICARE-Summer-Newsletter July-2013.pdf.

[5] Tucker, Karen Iris. 2014. "How Angelina Jolie Changed Things For People With *BRCA* Mutations." The Forward. https://forward.com/culture/204221/how-angelina-jolie-changed-things-for-people-with/.

[6] Boggs MD, Will. 2017. "Do Patients and Doctors Understand Breast Cancer Genetic Testing Results?" Reuters.com. https://www.reuters.com/article/us-health-breastcancer-genetic-testing/do-patients-and-doctors-understand-breast-cancer-genetic-testing-results-idUSKBN17L2MG.

[7] Otten, Ellen, et al. "Telegenetics Use in Presymptomatic Genetic Counselling: Patient Evaluations on Satisfaction and Quality of Care." *European Journal of Human Genetics* 24, no. 4 (2016): 513–20. PMC Web. February 24, 2018.

OTHER SOURCES

Buchanan, Adam H., Santanu K. Datta, Celette Sugg Skinner, Gail P. Hollowell, Henry F. Beresford, et al. December 2015. "Randomized Trial of Telegenetics vs. In-Person Cancer Genetic Counseling: Cost, Patient Satisfaction and Attendance." *Journal of Genetic Counseling* 24, no. 6: 961–70. https://search.proquest.com/openview/72ba5d981d7be0745fe4777f652491e5.

PART X. BUTTERFLIES AND BLOOMS

CHAPTER 24: SURPRISE LILY

[1] "Surgery to Reduce the Risk of Breast Cancer." n.d. National Cancer Institute. https://www.cancer.gov/types/breast/risk-reducing-surgery-fact-sheet.

[2] Zalewski, Shelley. 2016. "Choosing Double Mastectomy, Even if Not Medically Necessary." Blog. Lab Blog, University Of Michigan Health. http://labblog.uofmhealth.org/lab-report/choosing-double-mastectomy-even-if-not-medically-necessary.

[3] "Contralateral Breast Cancer Risk in *BRCA1* and *BRCA2* Mutation Carriers." *Journal of Clinical Oncology* 27, no. 35 (December 2009): 5862–64. https://doi.org/10.1200/JCO.2009.25.1652.

CHAPTER 25: NAKED LADY LILIES

[1] Jung, Carl. 1955. "Synchronicity: An Acausal Connecting Principle." *In The Collected Works of C. G. Jung*, vol. 8.

The twins—Mom and Aunt Marilyn

Best friends Norene and Mom

Best friends Amy and Char

Kristin

Kristin and Amy

Amy and "Sista" Jan

Amy and Dad circa 1974

Amy and Dad July 2, 2000

Jon and Amy

Lillian and Bo

Lillian and Dad

Lillian